ANYONE SEEN MY ROSE-COLORED GLASSES?

GOD'S WORD IN EVERYDAY LIFE

Written by:
Regina Stone Matthews

Illustrated by:
Donna Brown

Copyright © 2017 Atwater & Bradley Publishers
All rights reserved.
Regina Stone Matthews

ISBN-13: 978-0692929193
ISBN-10: 0692929193

All Scripture quotations, unless otherwise indicated are taken from the Holy Bible, New International Version®, NIV® Copyright ©1973, 1978, 1984, 2011 by Biblica, Inc.® Used by permission. All rights reserved worldwide.

For my husband David, my knight in shining armor who loves me unconditionally and taught me the meaning of perseverance.

I love you to the moon and back.

ACKNOWLEDGEMENTS

TO THE ONE WHO guides me and loves me regardless of my shortcomings. The One who allows me the freedom, honor, and pleasure to write—my Lord and my Savoir Jesus Christ. May I make You proud in all I do.

To my family: David, Sandi, Tim, Danielle, Skye, Dylan, Noel, Kevin, Ashlee, Jeremie, and Haylie. To my parents, Claude and Evelyn, who are forever in my heart and share God's kingdom together. I love you all beyond measure.

To my super talented illustrator, Donna Brown, whose support and patience is never ending and forever appreciated. Thank you my dear friend.

To my editor, Anne Mateer, a gifted writer and editor whose advice I cherish. Who always guided me in the direction I may not have wanted to go, but needed to go. Thank you my dear friend.

Psalm 139:1–5

TABLE OF CONTENTS

My Life as a Toilet Paper Roll Changer	1
I Still Remember When We Used to Dance in the Den	13
Papa's Kitchen, Where the Half Matters	21
Anticipating Emma	31
The Day George Bailey Came to Visit	37
I Never Knew Tyler	49
What Good Ever Came Out of Being Broke?	57
Things Our Mothers Used To Tell Us	69
I Never Did Like Dogs Anyway	79
Miss Fields Was a Tough Old Bird	91
Skye for President	101
The Reason Doing it My Way Doesn't Work	117
Ella	125
When Mr. Matthews Went to Washington: In Honor of Technical Staff Sergeant Byron Waitcel Matthews	135
God Gave Me Friends So I Wouldn't Have to Deal with Harriet Oleson	143
Dare to Tell the Truth	153
My Daddy's Truck	161
Remembering Will Have to Do	171
Where In the World Did that Hair on My Chin Come From?	181
Where Exactly Are the Places You Will Go?	191

INTRODUCTION

WE EXPERIENCE SO MUCH throughout our lives. Lessons learned and all that. But do we? Learn our lessons, I mean. And where does God fit into it all? If there even is a God, some might say. I believe there most certainly is a God. I believe He gave us His Word to guide us through this life. But if we're looking for fluff or political correctness or the ever-popular *feel good* stuff all the time, well, maybe we ought to stick to reading fairy tales. But guess what? Fairy tales aren't honey and sugar all the time either. You know that bed of roses thing? Funny thing about roses. They have thorns. Remember *Sleeping Beauty*? How about *Snow White*? Then there's *Cinderella*. I'm sure they'd all tell us they never saw any rose petals on the ground while making their way to the altar. It's the happily ever after we seem to crave. Still, we must learn how to deal with the harshness that goes with it. Which begs the question—how does the Bible relate to all of this?

Psalm 19:7–14 tells us that the Scripture is sufficient for our lives. It is "perfect, refreshing the soul." Scripture is "right, giving joy to the heart," and "radiant, giving light to the eyes." Furthermore, Scripture is "pure, enduring forever" and "firm and altogether righteous." Making it "more precious than gold." What a wonderful way to look at God's Word.

I've always read the Bible *very* slowly. Mainly because it can be so complex, and I am not so complex. I make every effort to be in a quiet place with no distractions so I can carefully and prayerfully understand the message. Second Timothy 3:16 says it best, "All Scripture is God-breathed and is useful for teaching, rebuking, correcting and training in righteousness," which makes it even more important to be mindful of the fact that God's Word is eternal.

Some say the Bible no longer applies in today's world. I'd argue against that point. I believe the Bible is here to stay, regardless of the topic. Regardless of the century. More importantly, regardless of whether or not it is believed.

Within these pages you'll find a collection of stories dealing with all sorts of things that drive us mad. From abortion to suicide. From stubbornness to drugs, sex, and rock 'n roll. From racism to friends to that all-important topic of the toilet paper roll changer. There's the family dog, Harriet Oleson, George Bailey, telling the truth, memories, teachers, redneck trucks and so much more. Then I throw the Bible into the mix to irritate the atheists. I know, it's cruel to purposely set out to irritate folks. But sometimes it's necessary.

Some of my stories are funny, some sad, some controversial. All are told with humor, seriousness, and a bit of sarcasm. Now don't get put off by that word *sarcasm*. What would life be without a touch of it, right? It's like that hit of hot spice in the back of the throat after eating a savory dish.

And every story is entirely from my point of view.

Who am I? Well, I'm just me. I'm not famous or even well-known. I am one person who decided to take off my rose-colored glasses and write about those every day, real-life things that God's Word speaks to so very clearly.

But be prepared. The Bible doesn't mince words. Nor does it take care not to offend. And yet it most often gives the reader a fulfillment of the soul that brings comfort to those who dare to simply read.

It is my sincere prayer that at the end of this book you'll come to the realization that God's Word will never be obsolete no matter the year or century. Just like His love for us will never end.

CHAPTER ONE

My Life as a Toilet Paper Roll Changer

THROUGHOUT MY CHILDHOOD, I dreamt of becoming a famous singer. Never mind I couldn't carry a tune in a bucket. I figured since my mother could sing, it only stood to reason I could also. Why not dream big, I always say. So I sang everywhere I went. I never realized what this did to the listener. I even joined the church choir. To this day I'm amazed they actually allowed me to sing. Looking back on it, they probably just felt sorry for me because I tried so hard.

There were enough good singers in the choir to cover over my singing. It's always reminded me of the *Andy Griffith Show* episode when the town choir loses its tenor. They are in need of a replacement, and the choir director discovers Barney sings tenor. Only Barney is a terrible singer. The whole choir is upset over how his singing disrupts choir practice. They want him gone. Of course, it's up to Andy to break the news to Barney.

I was Barney. Only, I didn't have a friend like Andy to let me down easy.

After finally realizing stardom via the vocal route would never happen, I turned my sights to yet another occupation—dancing. I saw myself as a world-renowned ballerina! I remember reading about Anna Pavlova. She became famous for her portrayal of a swan in *The Dying Swan*. She delivered a beautiful performance. Margot Fonteyn and Maria Tallchief were both extraordinary ballerinas. I admired their talent.

And who could forget the guys? Mikhail Baryshnikov (my personal favorite) and Rudolf Nureyev, both amazingly talented. Of course, I read about Nureyev during my teenage years. Baryshnikov came along during my early twenties.

Unable to strike a pose on my toes, my mother enrolled me in tap-dancing classes. All my mother's friends said, "She's so cute in her tap costume." I actually have pictures to prove that statement.

Cute as I might be, tap dancing didn't like me one little bit. I didn't dance very well at all, but my parents cheered me on in recitals, always giving me standing ovations much to the chagrin of the other parents who obviously thought I stunk. In the end, I hung up my tap shoes vowing never to tap again.

Now that singing and dancing were out, I decided to embark on a most auspicious venture—acting. I envisioned my name in lights at the local theatre house. Broadway even. I could hear the audience chanting my name. Directors, writers, producers all clamoring at the chance for me to appear in one or more of their productions. This must be my future—a world famous actress.

I immediately enrolled in acting classes and joined the drama club at school. I actually performed in a few plays. Katharine Hepburn, Grace Kelly, Elizabeth Taylor, Natalie Wood, Audrey Hepburn, Bette Davis all became role models for what I considered the beginning of my career as a famous actress. But, yet again, my talent fell short. I guess it makes for a not so favorable impression when you forget your lines. Like singing and dancing, acting took a back seat to things that turned out to be more my forte.

Throughout the years, I envisioned different occupational avenues that went from one end of the spectrum to the other. On my short list were occupations such as doctor, lawyer, teacher, Supreme Court Judge, TV News Anchor, etc. It never occurred to me I'd become something else, that the choices I made would ultimately catapult me into a lifelong career as a toilet paper roll changer.

I'm convinced someone who hated me chose this career on my behalf. One would think I could get off this path on my own accord. Nevertheless, here I've stayed.

During my lowest points, I concede to the fact that changing toilet paper rolls is what I was put on earth to do. The thing that makes it all so very sad is that I have no idea how it all began. One day, many years ago, I decided to sit down and write out how this fate of mine transpired. It went something like this . . .

My husband and I met.

That's it! Not really, but it began with that. It started out as a blind date. My best friend happened to be dating my future husband's roommate. These guys laid claim to being two savvy bachelors who thought themselves the cream of the crop.

One day my friend told me she met her guy's roommate. She thought I should meet him. Maybe I should even go out with him. "He has great teeth," she said.

Great teeth—seriously? Yeah, well, teeth were important to her.

I hated blind dates, so I only agreed to a phone call. He called. Oddly enough, we talked for two hours. Nice voice. If his looks matched his voice, now that would be sweet. I agreed to a date, but first we made a pact. If I didn't like what I saw when I opened the door, I could close it in his face. If he didn't like what he saw when I opened the door, he could walk away. With that said, we made the date. Did I mention I hated blind dates?

From the time I discovered this would not be a typical date, I knew my life would take a strange turn. We went to a *middle school* football banquet. Don't even laugh. Okay, go ahead. His roommate coached football and, coincidentally, the blind date fell on the same night as the banquet.

Now, the guys claimed they *really* wanted to hear the keynote speaker. I submit they *really* wanted to take advantage of the free food. I mentioned I hated blind dates, right?

The big night arrived. Keeping in mind the pact we made over the phone, I decided to play a trick on my unsuspecting blind date. The guys picked us up at my friend's apartment, and when I opened the door, I took one look at my guy and promptly closed the door in his face. I laughed and laughed. When I opened the door again, my date had walked away! And that's what is known as the beginning of an everlasting relationship.

From that point on, my husband and I share a somewhat silly partnership. At the beginning, we played multiple practical jokes on each another. The first time I met his family comes to mind. We were beginning to get serious, talking about marriage and all that goes with it. We were clearly out of our minds.

My husband, then boyfriend, decided it was time for me to meet the family. He'd met my family which consisted of a mother and a father. I'm an only child. He, on the other hand, had a mother and a father and a sister and a brother, four strangers for me to meet. Plus I needed to act as though I liked them, even if I didn't. I agreed to the meeting.

There are two food items I hate most in the world—fried fish and strawberry shortcake. Don't even start with me about strawberry shortcake.

Unbeknownst to me, my boyfriend, when asked by his mother what kind of food I liked, lied. "She loves fried fish and strawberry shortcake! They're her favorites!" What a creep.

The dreaded night drew near. My nerves were on end. Keep in mind I didn't know about my boyfriend's despicable trap.

The mom, the dad, the brother, and the sister turned out to be very nice people. I started wondering if my boyfriend might be adopted, because I knew him to be a wild and crazy guy prone to practical jokes. These lovely people seemed normal.

We sat around and chatted in an effort to get to know one another, when suddenly his mom called us to dinner. I saw this evil little twinkle in his eye. That should have been my first clue. It typically didn't take me long to bust him whenever he played one of his practical jokes, but my nerves overrode my brain and the evil little twinkle never registered.

We went into the dining room. The biggest platter of fried fish I'd ever seen in my entire life sat in the middle of the dining room table. I vomited in my mouth.

My boyfriend stood ever so proudly by my side with the biggest smile on his face. His mother said, "David told me how much you love fried fish." I vomited in my mouth again.

It took all my strength to smile, nod, and say, "Yum." I knew if I looked over at the guy I planned to one day call my husband, I would go for his jugular. That probably would end my relationship with his family, too, so I contained myself.

I made it through the fried fish and managed not to eat one bite. Fortunately, his mother served rice, too, which made it possible for me to choose the smallest fish, pick it apart and snuggle it ever so carefully under the rice. I hid the fish so well she asked if I wanted more. "I just couldn't eat another bite," I said.

With dinner over, I breathed a sigh of relief. I relished in the fact that I overcame a seemingly insurmountable obstacle. I foiled the despicable plot. The pride I felt didn't last long. His mother brought out dessert—the biggest strawberry shortcake known to mankind.

I looked over at my soon-to-be *ex*-boyfriend. He couldn't contain himself any longer. Cheeks flushing, tears rolling down his face, spit spewed in all directions out of his mouth. Disgusting! His mom smiled. "David told me how much you loved strawberry shortcake."

She then proceeded to cut me a piece of the revolting dish. With nothing on my plate to hide this stuff under, I took a deep breath and tried not to punch the evildoer in the nose. What in the world went through this woman's mind? Didn't she know she should serve a side dish with strawberry shortcake? Defeat loomed. I sat there and ate the horrible dessert this sweet, hospitable woman prepared with loving hands.

By the time I finished the cake, the evil villain had fallen out of his chair laughing. From that point on I knew silliness would fill our relationship. (Just in case you're wondering, I never told his mother how much I hated that dinner.)

As time passed, we continued dating and actually married, despite that awful dinner. Eventually, the children came. Some might point to that as the turning point for my future career. I, on the other hand, find it deplorable to blame children for anything other than stretch marks. Oh, and morning sickness. Wait—and hemorrhoids. Then again there are droopy boobs and a lifetime of getting rid of all the baby fat. And grey hair, laryngitis from screaming, not to mention dark circles and bags under the eyes from lack of sleep over these people. The sense of smell is never the same again either.

Most likely both—husband and kids—opened the door for my career as a toilet paper roll changer. These people use the bathroom constantly. It only stands to reason a household filled with these types would run out of toilet paper on a regular basis. Somewhere along the line I became the designated toilet paper roll changer. Why? All I know is one day I'm dreaming of life as a famous singer, dancer, actress, Supreme Court Judge, and the next day I'm a toilet paper roll changer.

After years of constantly being the only one in my house with the knowledge, skill and experience in the art of toilet paper roll changing, I decided to wait them out by not doing my job.

To my dismay, I heard things like, "Mom! Can you bring me a roll of toilet paper! Someone left it empty and didn't even bother to change it, and now I'm stuck! Mom! Did you hear me? Mom!"

Or, "Honey, would you mind bringing me a roll of toilet paper! Ha! Ha! Ha! I didn't realize the roll was empty. Ha! Ha! Ha! Did you hear me? Honey? Ha! Ha! Ha!"

After coming to their aid, do they actually think to change out the empty roll with the full one I handed them? Nope. They leave the new roll sitting on top of the empty roll.

They knew I would not be capable of leaving it that way. They knew I would change it out. There's no defense for this except to say I'm a dope.

It grieves me to share how low I stooped in an effort to sway my family over to my way of thinking regarding empty toilet paper rolls. I cleverly stripped down the toilet paper roll to one single solitary little square of toilet paper just hanging there begging for someone to come along and refill it with a brand new roll. Then I patiently waited until one of them went into the bathroom. I wanted to see how they would handle the situation. Most sane people would notice the lack of toilet paper, and would get a roll before they sat down, right?

Yet they continued on with their business with *no* toilet paper, I don't know why I thought having only one square in play would change matters. About the only thing I can say in their defense is that I know for a fact they washed their hands.

At that moment, I finally resolved that it was my destiny in life to change the toilet paper roll for my family.

In an effort to make some sense of this most egregious situation, I spoke with other mothers in my neighborhood to see if, like me, they were saddled with this despicable task. Much to my delight, they, too, held the role of designated toilet paper roll changers in their households.

Armed with this knowledge, I no longer felt alone in this pit known as *The Toilet Paper Abyss*. Just knowing others held my same position made the load that much easier to bear. What a wonderful feeling. I no longer found myself plotting the demise of my family. I returned the firecrackers and cherry bombs I thought of planting inside the toilet bowl. Life seemed easier and more pleasant now that I accepted my role in society. Although quite without glamour and most commonplace, I find it to be a much needed position.

If truth be known, we wear many hats while living with and raising our families. Some are fun to wear. Some are not. We wear them nonetheless because we love our families more than we love ourselves. That's how it should be.

We all know the verse in 2 Corinthians 9:7: "Each of you should give what you have decided in your heart to give, not reluctantly or under compulsion, for God loves a cheerful giver." That helps put what we do for our families and for others into perspective.

When I think of my family, I think of all the happiness and all the sadness that touched each of us. It brings me peace to know we shared these times together.

A favorite message of mine in the Bible is 1 Corinthians 13:1–13. Here's a sample of what it tells us in verses 1, 3, 11, and 13: "If I speak in the tongues of men or of angels, but do not have love, I am only a resounding gong or a clanging cymbal . . . If I give all I possess to the poor and give over my body to hardship that I may boast, but do not have love, I gain nothing . . . When I was a child, I talked like a child, I thought like a child, I reasoned like a child. When I became a man, I put the ways of childhood behind me . . . And now these three remain: faith, hope and love. But the greatest of these is love." Simply beautiful.

So life has come full circle. It began with the changing out of toilet paper rolls when my family was young and continued to the changing out toilet of paper rolls now that my family is older.

I guess there are some things that really never do change.

As I look back over the times when my aspirations were higher—world-famous singer, ballet dancer, actress, doctor, lawyer, Supreme Court Justice, TV news anchor, and the like—I find myself laughing out loud. All quite possibly within my reach, except for the singer, ballet dancer, or actress. Clearly the world is better off without being subjected to my inept skills in such talent-required careers. It's fun to dream, though. And I like to think God sees a much grander plan for me some day.

In the meantime, while waiting for those plans to unfold, I decided it's not all that bad that I find myself in a career I never thought I would occupy. Even without the talent required to fulfill all the careers I once dreamt of, I have a family I love more than I love myself. God blessed me with a group of remarkable people who just happen to be my husband, children, and grandchildren.

Where we begin in life and where we end up holds many surprises. In my case, when all is said and done, I'm really not so unhappy with my life as a toilet paper roll changer.

CHAPTER TWO

*I Still Remember When We
Used to Dance in the Den*

WHEN I HEAR THE song "Brown Eyed Girl," I immediately think of a particular dance at my high school. The guy I dated at the time belonged to a band that played the song. He always dedicated it to me. Oh, the gah-gah of it all. He definitely had me at hello. Now when listening to the Golden Oldies station and "Brown Eyed Girl" comes on, I think of that dance and that guy. I wonder whatever happened to him and how the time slipped by so quickly.

We all possess memories of times we cherish and times that make us sad. Calling to mind the joyful times seems easy. We remember, we smile, and probably laugh. Then some memories we push away. Bringing them to mind causes us pain, sadness, or even anger. No matter the memories, we really can't escape them.

I've often wondered how many memories I either lost or simply pushed so deep down inside that their mere existence seems impossible. Painful memories find their way to the surface at times when we least expect them. They can seep out of our pores undetected.

How we react to situations sometimes stems from a memory. They surface when someone pushes the right (or wrong) button. It calls to mind a memory that's been carefully tucked away into the recesses of the brain. When we dream we sometimes bring into our dreams those memories we chose to forget. Recalling one's past is a complicated thing.

I'm amazed by how sounds and smells trigger a memory in an instant. Moreover, the memory comes to mind in its entirety. There's no selective process involved. Like a flash of light, good memories appear right along with the bad.

Smells bring back many memories for me. The smell of bread baking makes me think of my daddy. Onion rings frying make me think of the Varsity—a drive-in restaurant located in Atlanta,

Georgia, where, every teenager within a hundred miles used to gather on the weekends. The special smell of Aramis cologne makes me think of my husband.

So many types of memories fill our minds. Good and bad. Funny and sad. We relive them over and over, cleaving to a time when the memory was reality.

For me, dancing in the den is one of those memories. When I bring to mind this special time, one of two reactions occurs. The first is one of longing. The second is one of angst. Sounds like a memory one wouldn't want to remember. Not really. It's a bit of a bitter-sweet recall that, although it brings me joy, the joy produces longing. The longing, in turn, produces angst.

When our children were small, life took on a hectic tone. My husband and I both worked forty plus hours a week. With three kids, a mortgage, a dog, food and clothing to buy, and car loans to pay, how else does one survive? So on and on it went. Gathering the kids together after work, getting them home, getting them fed, and ready for bed made for what seemed like another forty-plus hours that we obviously pulled out of thin air. Memory doesn't serve me well at this point, because for the life of me I can't recall how we accomplished such a feat.

As our kids grew older, the addition of school changed the equation. Bear in mind we still worked the forty-plus hours a week. We still went through the ritual of gathering the kids together, getting them home, and fed. But now homework needed tackling and *finally* bed. Where, in all that's sane in this world, did we find the time to do all this stuff?

Regardless, it worked like a well-oiled machine. Insanity doesn't begin to cover how our lives evolved from day to day. I can only come up with super human strength as a possible answer. Now it takes me an hour just to get out of bed, eat a bowl of cereal, and drink a cup of coffee. Plus another hour to get a shower, get dressed, and my bed isn't made yet! I digress.

I do remember this. On Friday nights after the kids were asleep, my husband and I would go downstairs, turn on the stereo ever so softly, and, in the twilight, we'd slow dance in the den. It was magical. Nothing else existed in the world. Every stress drifted away with the sound of the music. When I think of that special time, I envision two silhouettes floating across the floor. We felt as light as air in each other's arms as the music carried us to a more peaceful place. Two souls joined as one. Did I mention it was magical?

We worked our guts out and grabbed every second of down time possible in an effort to make a glorious memory. I cherish every second we shared together in that den, dancing with each another, and loving one another so very much. What bothers me about this particular memory is the pain it brings to my heart and the longing it brings to my soul. Special or happy memories pull at our heart-strings because the moment no longer exists. It can't be recaptured. I ache for that time when life seemed so very simple, never mind the day-to-day chaos of work and kids.

Worries? Of course. Stress? Of course. Craziness? Of course. But what didn't exist were the worries, stress, and craziness we find ourselves experiencing in today's culture. Sad but true.

I challenge anyone to walk down the street and ask someone over the age of fifty to recall a memory from his or her past. Odds are they'd recall a simplistic memory. They'd smile—laugh even. Then there'd be a brief moment of wistfulness. That bit of melancholy that leaves us longing and yearning for a time gone by, when life seemed simple and uncomplicated.

I submit we hold our memories closer to our hearts than anything we own because they validate our existence. We ponder them and learn from them. We laugh over them and cry over them.

We even try to forget the ones that tear us apart. But no matter what the memory, they shape us.

The Bible, from what I can determine, doesn't speak to our human memory as we define the word. But I do know that in Luke 1:1–4, Luke, the author and a physician by trade, speaks of writing things down in an orderly fashion so that those who read the accounts of the past—the memories of the author—would be certain of the occurrences. The passage reads like this: "Many have undertaken to draw up an account of the things that have been fulfilled among us, just as they were handed down to us by those who from the first were eyewitnesses and servants of the word. With this in mind, since I myself have carefully investigated everything from the beginning, I too decided to write an orderly account for you, most excellent Theophilus, so that you may know the certainty of the things you have been taught."

This is probably why we keep journals and diaries, or write letters. It helps us to remember facts as they occurred or as they were taught to us. It also allows us to later recall days gone by. Our memories come to life when we write them down.

My husband enjoys talking about his past and all the fun times of his youth. I'm up for that sometimes, but I enjoy more sharing memories of my kids and the fun times with them. The memories we're making with our grandchildren are especially wonderful. But I do experience times of nostalgia. I recall the times of my childhood and my crazy adolescent days. Those memories often bring a laugh or two—or three or four.

At times I even find myself drifting off into a memory-filled dreamland and landing in that time when I possessed a lot more energy, despite my busy days. I think I probably smiled and laughed more.

Things seem overly serious nowadays. We're bombarded with

bad news at every turn. Makes you wish you'd never heard of 24/7 news cycles. And we thought a thousand channels to choose from would be so cool.

So when I think I'm getting bogged down in the misery of it all, I reach into the past—and yes, after all these years, I still remember when we used to dance in the den.

CHAPTER THREE

*Papa's Kitchen,
Where the Half Matters*

I T'S DIFFICULT FOR ME to believe that my daddy passed away over twenty years ago. The harsh pain subsided with time; the mourning finally ended as the memories of a life fully lived emerged.

His parents named him Claude Calloway Stone. I called him Daddy. My kids called him Papa. Throughout his life he held many positions—chef, semi-pro baseball player, drill sergeant, restaurant owner and school teacher, to name a few. To his family, undoubtedly the best cook the world ever knew. I think he loved cooking more than he loved anything.

I can close my eyes and literally smell the aromas that floated in, around, and out of my daddy's kitchen. He never used a recipe, but wrote many. He never needed to measure anything; he knew exactly how much each recipe required. He said, "If you're following a recipe, *never* change it or substitute anything, because the half matters."

The military knew the value of my daddy as their mess hall sergeant before he became a drill sergeant. Some might say they are one in the same. My bet is he will go down in history as the best chef Fort Jackson, South Carolina, ever employed—past, present, and future. He went on to become a master sergeant before he retired years later.

In the 1970's, he and my mother moved to the North Georgia Mountains and opened a restaurant outside the town of Helen. They called it *The Delcliff*. Hugely successful, pulling in folks from all over the state. After several years of running the restaurant, they sold it and moved back to Atlanta. If you've never worked in the food industry, let me just make this point—it's without a doubt the hardest work you'll ever do. It's back-breaking, feet-aching, gut-sweating, and sometimes heart-breaking work that runs 24/7 with sixteen tons of responsibility. My daddy loved every second of it. You must, or it will literally kill you.

Time plays dirty little tricks on us. Age, and all that goes with it, sneaks up behind us when we're not looking and brings us to our knees. So the decision to sell the restaurant emerged. The family rejoiced because now *we* were his customers. There would be more time for him to cook just for us.

Some of our favorite things were Daddy's yeast rolls, cinnamon rolls, and breads. When Papa cooked, we all showed up. But when yeast rolls were on the menu, I could be found standing in front of the oven, knife in one hand, a pound of butter in the other, drooling all over myself. I pity the poor soul who even attempted to step in front of me.

Daddy would laugh, "Now don't run me over before I get them out of the oven. There will be plenty of time to suck them down." And suck them down we did, like a pack of mad dogs—with me leading the pack! My mouth waters just thinking of them.

After Daddy died, I wondered where he kept the recipe for those yeast rolls. He never let me, or anyone for that matter, in the kitchen while cooking certain things, so I never saw how he made them. The ingredients for his rolls, breads, pastas, and sauces were never shared with anyone. Not even my mother. I hoped he left a note or something behind as to the location of his coveted recipes. No such luck. We finally gave up the search.

When my mother made the decision to sell her house and move to Texas to live with us, I hoped I might find at least one of his hand-written recipes tucked away somewhere. He had written down those recipes he didn't mind sharing. I prayed the recipe for his yeast rolls might be among them.

Daddy owned at least two million cookbooks. I don't know why. He never used them. He never *needed* to use them. Some of them my mother used. I think he just bought them because he thought chefs should have cookbooks in their kitchens. So when we were cleaning out the house, I went through every single one of his cookbooks in the hopes of finding a hand-written recipe folded inside the pages. Nope. It left me heartsick—and a part of me got really miffed. He didn't leave one recipe behind? I'm his daughter, after all. What was he thinking?

My oldest daughter and I divided up the cookbooks. Those we didn't want went in the yard sale. I decided not to brood about it. What would be the point? Taking his secrets to the grave was just like him.

Daddy always made his special breads and rolls at Thanksgiving and Christmas. I hoped I could continue the tradition. It created a bit of an obstacle with no recipe. Not that I thought I could duplicate in any way what he produced. Baking breads and rolls from scratch tends to bring on anxiety attacks and strange-looking rashes all over my body. So I guess it really didn't matter after all that he never left me the recipes. I'm sure I would have made a mess of them. But somehow the holidays wouldn't be the same.

After we sold my mother's house and she settled into ours, I started unpacking the boxes of things we'd kept. Mother brought along her fold-out recipe box. It held a collection of the favorite recipes she prepared throughout her marriage.

One Thanksgiving, I suddenly wondered, *what if Daddy put his yeast roll recipe in Mother's recipe box?* What if he put his cinnamon roll recipe, spaghetti sauce recipe, and Swedish meatball recipe in there, too? It was too much to hope for. I went through every single compartment of that box. Not one single hand-written recipe from Daddy showed its face. I got miffed all over again. What was he thinking?

Many Thanksgivings and Christmases passed since my initial reaction to my daddy not leaving behind any of his recipes. With the arrival of each holiday, I reminisced about the smells and flavors that came out of Daddy's kitchen, all the while wishing he'd taken the time to write out the instructions and the secret ingredients to his mouth-watering dishes.

Then one year, my middle daughter decided she wanted my mother and me to make my aunt's sixteen-layer chocolate cake for her birthday—a task that requires two people. My mother always made the cake without following the recipe because she'd made it so many times before. But after ninety-plus years of living, she could no longer remember the exact ingredients or the exact measurements, which are important when baking. She lamented she never wrote it down, and therefore, I wouldn't find it among her recipes. Not to worry. I knew I could find it on my computer or in my recipe box. (I do still keep a few recipes in a special box I've owned for years. Guess it's a way of hanging on to life before computers.)

Having no success locating the recipe on my computer, I turned to my recipe box. As I began looking through the collection, my eyes caught a glimpse of several pieces of paper neatly folded and tucked away in the very back. Funny, I'd never seen them there before. But, then, I rarely went through the box anymore.

A feeling of nervousness I couldn't explain suddenly came over me as I reached to retrieve the neatly folded pieces of paper in the back.

Their yellowish hue caught my eye immediately. They didn't appear brittle, so I knew they couldn't be that old, but I still felt compelled to take care as I gently handled them.

The papers were folded in half and then folded again. As I opened the first fold, I could see it was something handwritten. As I opened the second fold, I recognized the handwriting. Tears began to roll down my face even before I read the first word. My heart already knew what the pages contained.

I closed my eyes. When I opened them again I saw the words, "Yeast Rolls" on the first page. On the second page, "Cinnamon Rolls." On the third page, "Sauces." On the fourth page, "Breads."

Daddy's recipes. Four of the things he made that I loved the most. He'd taken the time to leave behind a piece of himself. Something special and close to his heart. What had *I* been thinking?

I couldn't imagine when he'd put the recipes in the box. The color of the paper put the time over twenty years. I sat there staring at the pages, going back in my mind trying to figure out when Daddy would have had access to my recipe box. Maybe the day we moved from Atlanta to Dallas, during all the chaos. Maybe the last time he visited us after we moved. I thought and thought. When?

One particular Christmas gave me pause. He made the yeast rolls while I stood in my usual place—right in front of the oven. I remember asking him if he would give me the recipe, or at least let me watch him make them. He answered with a resounding no. I knew he meant it, and so I gave it up.

At that time, my husband and I had been married only a couple of years. Long time ago. We invited my parents over to our apartment for Christmas dinner. I decided that must have been it. I can only imagine him sneaking into my kitchen, making sure no one could see him, and then carefully placing the coveted recipes in the box. He knew I would find them eventually. I only wish I'd found them before he died. But then there wouldn't have been that TAH DAH moment, and Daddy lived for the TAH DAH moments.

For all of my daddy's discipline, sternness, and need for perfection, he couldn't help but be a big softy inside. And even though he said no 99 percent of the time, sometimes, on occasion, he gave in and said yes. I suspect that particular Christmas was one of those yes times.

He would never admit it, mind you, but as I look back on that day, his "no" sounded a little different, no matter how resounding it came across. Then there's the possibility he'd already put the recipes in the box before I asked.

Having exhausted my brain trying to narrow down the time-frame, I decided to simply accept the gift. And so I did—with great humbleness. I knew how much Daddy cherished his art of cooking, so I knew the magnitude of the gift. It's one I will cherish for the rest of my life.

After all my ranting about my daddy's unwillingness to share, the question then became: would I actually attempt to make the yeast rolls and the cinnamon rolls and the breads? Although I begged him to reveal his secrets, going so far as to bad-mouth him when he refused, the possibility of actually attempting to duplicate his work would probably never happen. Somehow living up to the legend isn't something I'll dare attempt.

Cooking is truly an art. Television is filled to overflowing with chefs, cooks, and bakers who dazzle our taste buds by first appealing to our eyes. As my daddy and all chefs will state, people eat with their eyes first, so it's all about the presentation.

Most things in life are about the presentation—the perception if you will. Therefore, when preparing any dish, how it's presented to the consumer is paramount to how the consumer will receive it. So when Daddy said one should never mess with the recipe, he meant it would mess with the final presentation. That's why he told me always to put the full measurement into whatever I happened to be making. Leaving out a portion of the ingredient would make for a not-so-presentable dish. The half matters.

This brings me to the point of my story. The half matters in our life. Our one-on-one or group relationships, our workplace, our beliefs—in everything. I've often wondered why people choose not to do their best. Why some believe it's better to forget the half. I submit it's merely easier. Let's face it, the *good stuff* ain't easy. If it were easy, it would be called indifference.

Just how much does the half matter? In Luke 16:19–26 we read: "There was a rich man who dressed in purple and fine linen and lived in luxury every day. At his gate was laid a beggar named Lazarus, covered with sores and longing to eat what fell from the rich man's table. Even the dogs came and licked his sores. The time came when the beggar died and the angels carried him to Abraham's side. The rich man also died and was buried. In Hades, where he was in torment, he looked up and saw Abraham far away, with Lazarus by his side. So he called to him, 'Father Abraham, have pity on me and send Lazarus to dip the tip of his finger in water and cool my tongue, because I am in agony in this fire.' But Abraham replied, 'Son, remember that in your lifetime you received your good things, while Lazarus received bad things, but now he is comforted here and you are in agony. And besides all this, between us and you a great chasm has been set in place, so that those who want to go from here to you cannot, nor can anyone cross over from there to us.'"

This story tells us in no uncertain terms that the half most certainly matters. Had the rich man taken that half step toward Lazarus while they were both still alive, things might have turned out differently.

As it is with indifference, we find there are no measurements, because being indifferent means you don't really care about the half. Proverbs 24:30–34 nails it when speaking to indifference and how the half just might matter: "I went past the field of a sluggard, past the vineyard of someone who has no sense; thorns had come up everywhere, the ground was covered with weeds, and the stone wall was in ruins. I applied my heart to what I observed and learned a lesson from what I saw: A little sleep, a little slumber, a little folding of the hands to rest—and poverty will come on you like a thief and scarcity like an armed man."

So, I guess my daddy was right all along. It's okay to guard your recipes. It's even okay not to share them. Unless, that is, you have a brat like me for a daughter, who hounds you every waking moment saying stupid things like, "Please, oh please, oh please! Can I have your recipes? Please, oh, please, oh please!" Which I'm sure he grew weary of hearing.

He did, however, decide to share. Something I never thought he would do. He put into action his lesson about cooking and making sure not to forget the half because it always matters. He made the effort, remembered the half mattering, and left behind a precious gift. But not before getting the last laugh on me. Thanks, Daddy.

There were many lessons my daddy attempted to instill in me. Some I listened to and some I blew off. Ultimately I regretted the lessons I didn't heed. For some reason, the half mattering stuck with me. Probably because the yeast rolls hung in the balance. I'm just glad I learned early to pay attention to the half. It's become a source of guidance throughout my life.

With all the drama subsided, I still remember the smells, the warmth, and the goodness that came from my daddy's kitchen. Or as my kids would say, "No, Mom, you mean Papa's kitchen—where the half matters!"

Luke 16:19-26
Proverbs 24:30-34

CHAPTER FOUR

Anticipating Emma

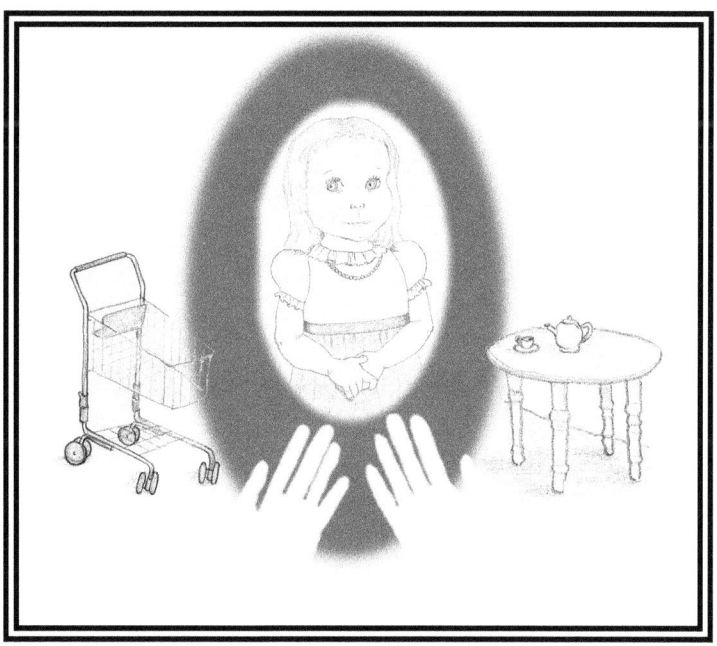

I ENJOY MANY BOOKS and movies. Some I like more than others. Some I love. Of all of them, *Emma* tops the list, both as my favorite book and movie.

Emma, a rich, spoiled, idealistic, young woman sees herself as the caretaker of those less fortunate than she. In an attempt to lead unsuspecting friends in the direction she feels best for them, she succeeds only in making matters worse. And yet throughout the story, Emma, regardless of her flaws, charms her way into your heart.

In spite of my attachment to Jane Austen's character Emma, the name itself always topped my list of favorite names. Which brings me to one particular day. It was dreadful.

My daughter and son-in-law had gathered our family together on a Sunday evening several weeks earlier to share with us the marvelous news that they were pregnant. Two home pregnancy tests solidified the happy fact.

This news brought the joy of knowing we'd soon hear the names Papa and Memaw echoing throughout our Texas home, the names our grandchildren in Georgia dubbed us years earlier. Georgia puts our current three grandchildren over a thousand miles away, making it impossible for us to visit more than once or twice a year. Having a baby in town to smooch on, spoil, and show off could not have come at a better time. Our oldest grandchild no longer required our doting as she had gone and grown up! How tacky. The news of a brand spanking new baby thrilled us to our souls. The anticipation set in before we could help ourselves.

With the doctor's appointments in place and the prenatal vitamins ordered, the anticipation grew. Talk about whether to find out the gender of the baby went back and forth. Some of us said yes, and some of us said no. The two most important people said yes. And so with the decision made to find out the baby's gender, the first doctor's appointment arrived. With it, however, came the unsettling news that although an amniotic sac had developed, the baby had not.

I said a prayer, hoping my grandchild inherited my precociousness by playing hide-and-seek with the sonographer. But my motherly instincts wouldn't let me go in that direction. I already knew all too well the pain of losing a grandchild, something I never wanted to experience again. Yet the memory of the events leading up to that loss tugged at me. Not wanting to let go, I fought back vigorously. But fear hung on. Finally, like my friend Emma, I just pushed the thought right out of my mind.

The doctor requested additional blood work to determine my daughter's HCG levels. In the meantime, life went on as usual. It tends to do that regardless of our protests.

While doing my weekly grocery shopping, a small bundle of cuteness dressed in enough lace and pearls to ensure her femininity crossed my path. She looked about three, but already she drove a shopping cart. Upon my complimenting her driving abilities, she immediately shot me a killer smile, ran over, threw her arms around me, and kissed me—SMACK—right on my cheek. Her mother couldn't believe her eyes. Her little cuteness, she said, had never done that before. I felt honored.

While standing in the checkout line, I heard, "Come back here! Emma! Emma!" I'd assumed my new little friend to be long gone by this time. When I turned, I saw the cute little face running toward her mother, lace and pearls flying. My heart melted.

Emma. My favorite name. My favorite book. My favorite movie. At that instant, I made the decision that my future granddaughter must be named Emma. It mattered not that I didn't even know if my daughter carried a little girl. Nor did it matter that I had no authority to name this child in the first place. Meeting Emma made me even more anxious to meet this new addition to our family.

From that moment on, every cute little bundle, every happy little face, took on the characteristics of Emma—the name I secretly gave my soon-to-be-born granddaughter. I found myself smiling at each little girl who passed by, all the while envisioning the fun times my Emma and I would share together. Tea parties and the like filled my head to overflowing. Before long, my anticipation kicked into full throttle, making it impossible to imagine anything less than a perfect baby girl. A perfect little Emma!

That Sunday I made the announcement to the family that I'd chosen a name for my new granddaughter. The family collectively laughed. I shared my story of meeting Emma at the grocery store to make my case. The family laughed again. My son-in-law offered up his appreciation for the time and thought I put into this decision, but he thought it best to wait until we knew for sure the baby's health and gender. I agreed—reluctantly.

With the results of the blood tests came the unhappy news that Emma had not, in fact, played hide-and-seek with the sonographer. Emma chose not to appear at all. The doctor said the chromosomes didn't form properly. The amniotic sac was empty. She felt confident that Mother Nature took over, causing a miscarriage. I couldn't disagree more. At some point, God took over. He made the decision to postpone Emma's appearance. But that's just my humble, uneducated, medical opinion.

We read in Jeremiah 1:5: "Before I formed you in the womb I knew you, before you were born I set you apart; I appointed you as a prophet to the nations." What powerful scripture. To know that God is with us from the very instant we are formed. To realize He touches our hearts with His love and that His love is available to us throughout our lives.

I've found comfort in this verse since the loss of my oldest daughter's child, Tyler. Now Emma and her cousin reside together in heaven, both sitting in the lap of Jesus. They could not be more real to me had I held them in my arms. For whatever reason, I shall never know that joy, that pleasure, or that honor of holding them here on this earth. I will, however, know the joy of anticipating Emma.

CHAPTER FIVE

The Day George Bailey Came to Visit

WHO COULD EVER FORGET George Bailey? *It's a Wonderful Life* airs over the Christmas holidays every single year. In fact, I think I speak for the entire nation when I say we are all getting a little sick and tired of George Bailey. Well, at least I am.

I've watched the movie about a hundred times. Yes, by my own doing. So why does it sound as if I'm complaining? At the time of my "I'm sick and tired of this stupid movie" rant I didn't know why I felt the urge to complain about it—I just did. No one said, "If you don't sit down in front of this TV and watch this movie, you will die a terrible death!" I watched it of my own free will.

Then one year I decided to boycott George Bailey and his stupid movie. For the next several years, each time it aired, I promptly changed the channel. So there! How do you like that, George Bailey? I'm in control. I decide. It's *my* life, not George's. I've always lived a wonderful life. Who needs him anyway? So I said goodbye to George Bailey and his stupid movie. Forever.

As typically happens throughout my life, just when I think I'm calling the shots, God steps in and says, "Not so fast, Miss Smarty Pants! You are not the boss of you. You are not the one in control. So listen up." And that's the day George Bailey came to visit.

Marietta, Georgia is a sweet, beautiful, peaceful little suburb of Atlanta. We lived there for many years and attended a church that encompassed all of our wants and needs. We loved the people, but most of all we loved the pastor. Rev. Charles Sineath was his name, and preaching was his game. You'll never find any better.

To say we participated in every aspect of this church was an understatement. We were raising our kids at the time, and they participated in it all, too. It was a wonderful life.

That is, it *was* a wonderful life. Until the day we moved to Texas due to my husband's work. Our emotions ran the gamut—sad, happy, scared, excited. All of it. But the reality of the move meant we must leave our church and travel into the unknown. So we gathered up all our belongings, including the kids—yes, it's necessary to take them along too—and we faced the future with heads held high. All the while in the back of my mind I wondered, *are there churches in Texas?*

I quickly learned that in Texas there's a church on every corner. If a person can't find a church in Texas, his bread ain't fully baked. It's truly an atheist's worst nightmare.

We settled into our new home, school, and work. Then we started looking for a church. One would think it an easy task, given all the churches to choose from. But alas, no. I can't remember how many churches we visited. I stopped counting after fifty.

Why were we having such a difficult time finding a church we liked? Finally, it dawned on us. We suffered from the dreaded disease know as the *Charles Sineath Syndrome.* It became apparent to us that we compared every pastor we heard to Charles.

Well, why shouldn't we be picky? We were the ones who'd be sitting in the pew listening to the guy up there. It was our lives. We were the boss of us. We controlled what we would and wouldn't listen to.

"Not so fast," a voice said. Yep, you know who. So we listened. As if we had a choice in the matter. Eventually we found a church, became involved and again it was a wonderful life.

Until the bishop transferred the pastor to another church.

What? Are you kidding me?

After he left, it just went right downhill. Not such a wonderful life anymore. We stopped going to church. We resolved within our minds that we had a right to do this. After all, we were the boss of us. We were in control. We decided what we would and wouldn't do and where we would and wouldn't go. It was our wonderful life, right?

Time passed, as it usually does. We became content in our wonderful life. Not going to church and not being involved seemed okay now because our kids were grown. We didn't really need to be involved in a church. We were still Christians. We certainly didn't need a church to tell us that. We still read our Bible. We still believed in God. We were good, decent, hard-working people. We didn't do bad things. We followed the rules. We gave to charities. We paid our taxes. We were kind to others. We didn't drive over the speed limit—well, not much, anyway. We were kind to animals. We had it under control. We were the boss of us. It was a wonderful life.

Until—the Real Boss entered, pressing upon our minds that we really did need to find a church home. With that, the search began once again. Thankfully, we found a church that seemed to meet all our needs.

We really liked the pastor and the people. We visited for a few months before deciding to take the big plunge and join. Now we go every Sunday.

I started volunteering in some ministries. We started tithing. As I looked at different organizations, everything seemed great. We came to the conclusion that it really was a wonderful life after all!

Until the holidays began. This pastor, whom I thought I liked, started a series of sermons on—you guessed it—George Bailey and *It's a Wonderful Life*. Except he named his series, *It's a Wonder Full Life*.

Cute.

Not!

We already know what I think of George Bailey and his wonderful life. I wasn't impressed with my pastor's attempt at a play on words, but I thought to myself, "I don't have anything else going on right now. I'll sit through the first sermon. If I don't like it, I'll just skip the series and come back when it's over." It's my decision, after all. I decide whether or not I stay. I'm the boss of me, right? Unbeknownst to me, God (the *Real* Boss) had plans for me that I knew nothing about.

The sermon started with the pastor saying a few things about it being a *Wonder Full Life*. That part seemed okay. I began to admit to the possibility of a hasty judgment of this upcoming series. Suddenly the lights went down, the screens lit up, and I found myself face-to-face with none other than George Bailey!

This guy—the one I called pastor—actually began showing clips of *It's a Wonderful Life*. I felt trapped! I couldn't get up and walk out. With the darkness of the sanctuary, falling flat on my face seemed quite possible. How could any human being endure this kind of torture? It's been my experience when I'm entertaining these kind of thoughts, when I'm resisting things that are happening in my life, God lovingly taps me on the shoulder and whispers in my ear, "I need you to pay attention now."

So I began listening. Not really. I didn't like George Bailey. He's a schmuck. The movie is sappy. I'd seen it five hundred times, and so my boycott remained in effect. Besides, George Bailey and his wonderful life seemed irrelevant to my life or anyone else's. And it certainly seemed inappropriate to be learning about it in church. I saw no need to stay seated. Everybody knows I'm the boss of me.

And yet I sat there through the entire series of sermons.

Believe it or not, I started to like George Bailey again. I even asked for the movie at Christmas. George and I became good friends. I believed I understood the message God wanted me to understand. I felt proud of myself. I told my husband, "It most definitely is a wonderful and a wonder full life after all." He agreed.

We humans get a bit caught up in ourselves when we think we've figured things out. This is a most unattractive character flaw. I doubt we'll ever change, but I believe it's something to definitely work toward.

I felt pretty good about myself. I overcame my hatred for George Bailey. I liked my pastor again. I found contentment with all things me. Until God tapped me on the shoulder and said, "I need you to pay attention now."

What? I already paid attention. I got it! I didn't need to pay attention again. It's a wonderful life remember?

Into the New Year, my husband and I were asked to help with Communion. Our church serves Communion the first Sunday of each month. We were excited about being asked and willingly offered our services. I looked at it as doing my part, participating and being a good church member. That's another one of those huge character flaws. The clinical term for it is *The Big Head*.

On Communion Sunday there's still a sermon. This particular Sunday one of the other pastors led the service. We sat up at the front of the church in the reserved section. You know—the VIP section. The section for the special people. The participating, doing-our-part-good-church-member section. I felt quite satisfied with myself and settled in to listen to the sermon.

Typically, I look over the bulletin before the service gets started, but because we were participating in the service, there wasn't time. Note to self: God has a sense of humor.

The pastor stepped up to the podium. The first words that came out of her mouth were the title of the sermon: "Are You Ready for the Blessings and the Troubles of the New Year?" In my mind's eye I saw the face of George Bailey. The caption under his face read, "I need you to pay attention now." What? Not again. I thought we were finished with George Bailey. I left the lessons of George Bailey safely tucked under the Christmas blankets. I didn't need to learn anything more about George Bailey. It's a wonderful life, remember?

I couldn't get up and walk out now. I was sitting in the reserved section. The VIP section. The section for the special people. The participating, doing-our-part-good-church-member section. A conspiracy lurked all around, I tell you. These people were deliberately trying to get me to hate George Bailey again. But for what purpose? It made no sense.

I opened my bulletin in search of the sermon title. Surely I heard her incorrectly. It's been known to happen. But there the words glared back at me, "Are you ready for the Blessings and the Troubles of the New Year?"

Clearly this topic meant nothing to me. I knew I had a wonderful life. Bring on the blessings. But troubles? What troubles? I decided not to listen to that part. Plus, the pastor had a smile on her face. In fact, she smiled during the entire sermon, happy and joyous. She talked about blessings with a smile. She talked about troubles with a smile.

Obviously, the troubles she spoke of weren't big troubles. They must be teeny-tiny, little troubles. Like a pimple or something. She couldn't be talking about life-altering troubles. I convinced myself that the troubles she spoke of were really just annoyances. It felt good to be back in control of my thoughts and my emotions again. Being the boss of oneself is a great feeling. Hey, it's a wonderful life, after all.

Group participation came next. You know the kind where you have to turn to the person sitting next to you (even if you don't know who they are) and repeat after the speaker. Don't like it. Never have; never will. Group participation is an embarrassing experience, especially when the words being repeated make everyone feel uncomfortable.

This pastor wanted to get me. I was certain of it. She said, "Turn to the person next to you" (this is where I always begin to sweat) "and ask, 'Are You Ready for the Blessings and the Troubles of the New Year?'"

You were supposed to let him or her answer.

Then she said, "Now turn to the person on the other side and repeat, 'Are You Ready for the Blessings and the Troubles of the New Year?'"

And again you were supposed to let them answer. What a dumb exercise.

Of course, I'm always ready—ready for the blessings. But I answered no to the troubles. I viewed the entire thing as a joke. I knew I could handle any sort of trouble. I decide how to react to things. I'm in control of my emotions. In fact, I'm in control of everything. Besides, this sermon didn't suggest real troubles. And I knew it didn't apply to me. What? Did George Bailey just appear again?

It's funny how things can change in a few days time. Just ask George Bailey. One day it's a wonderful life, and the next day it's: *are you ready for the troubles of the New Year!*

I couldn't say ready described me. God knew it. He knew it all along. That's why I needed to be reintroduced to George Bailey. When the lady from the church called and asked us to help with Communion, I picked that particular date because I needed to be there. God made certain of it.

Less than a week later, George Bailey came to visit.

I happened to be up in my husband's office doing the thing I hate most in life. No, it's not cleaning. It's getting our yearly papers in order to send to the accountant for income tax preparation. Talk about a double whammy in the works.

The phone rang. When I answered, I heard my husband's voice on the other end. One would need to know my husband to know that he rarely calls me during the work day. My caution antenna went on high alert.

"What's up?"

He told me his job might be *eliminated*. That's a nice, non-combative word companies use for *you probably will not have a job in a few weeks, so get ready to join the ranks of the unemployed.*

We sat there for what seemed an eternity. Silence is definitely *not* golden. It's terrifying. Suddenly it wasn't such a wonderful life. I wished for George Bailey's demise in that lake. I wished I'd never seen that stupid movie. Then I remembered some idiot saying all her emotions were under control. I remembered her saying how she could control her own life. Who said that? Oh yeah. Me.

Like a movie clip in front of my eyes, I saw George Bailey and heard a voice in the background saying loudly, "Are you paying attention now?" Then George Bailey laughed this hideously evil laugh.

The silence finally ended as I heard myself asking, "Are you okay?" What a dumb question. How could he be okay? But my husband is strong and decent, so naturally he said, "I'm fine." One might think that to be untrue. I knew, however, at the core of his being he couldn't be anything else but fine because, for him, that's where God lives. I, on the other hand, never quite mastered that type of centeredness. I'm a bit of a "let me kick your behind first, and then we'll talk" person. So naturally the first thing that ran through my mind during the terrible silence was "Who's responsible, and how can I get at 'em?" I didn't even care if they sent me to the pokey. I just wanted to maim somebody.

The next day, the day after George Bailey came to visit, and the day after *the troubles of the New Year*, my husband and I talked and talked and talked. It helped. But no plan emerged; only pieces of ideas that would eventually come together into one great plan. I was confident of that.

One might think there's cause for worry, but there shouldn't be. George Bailey and I never really hated each other. I'm paying attention now. God made certain of that.

I now recognize who the boss of me is, and it ain't me. Am I scared? I would be lying if I said no. Am I certain of who's in control? Absolutely. God takes us on trips through this life. We balk, we complain, we argue, and we don't pay attention. But if we're smart, we learn.

I've realized I need to be ready for the troubles because the blessings are easy. More importantly, I've learned that it *is* a wonderful life, and it *is* a wonder full life. God made certain of that also.

He reminded me of Matthew 6:25–34 as it so eloquently reads: "Therefore I tell you, do not worry about your life, what you will eat or drink; or about your body, what you will wear. Is not life more than food, and the body more than clothes? Look at the birds of the air; they do not sow or reap or store away in barns, and yet your heavenly Father feeds them. Are you not much more valuable than they? Can any one of you by worrying add a single hour to your life? And why do you worry about clothes? See how the flowers of the field grow. They do not labor or spin. Yet I tell you that not even Solomon in all his splendor was dressed like one of these. If that is how God clothes the grass of the field, which is here today and tomorrow is thrown into the fire, will he not much more clothe you—you of little faith? So do not worry, saying, 'What shall we eat?' or 'What shall we drink?' or 'What shall we wear?' For the pagans run after all these things, and your heavenly Father knows that you need them. But seek first his kingdom and his righteousness, and all these things will be given to you as well. Therefore do not worry about tomorrow, for tomorrow will worry about itself. Each day has enough trouble of its own." God, in all His infinite wisdom, made me see, understand, believe, and learn all that these verses convey.

I guess George and I really do share a lot in common. Wonderful and wonder full lives are hard to come by and should never be taken for granted. Giving in and letting God be the boss of us also helps. He does a much better job than we could ever do.

That alone deserves at least a *thank you* to both of my ministers who took the time to bring me the messages God wanted me to hear. They never knew God's plan for their messages. They just preached the sermon of the day. Within those messages, I learned to thank George, too, even though our relationship started out so very rocky.

As I look forward to dealing with whatever comes our way, I now know I must ask for God's strength and His guidance. I must listen when He speaks because He is the boss of me, and He always has my best interest at heart. Even though the times seem scary, God took care of us the day George Bailey came to visit.

CHAPTER SIX

I Never Knew Tyler

TYLER DAVID BERNARD DIED November 4, 1996. He was my grandson, and I never even knew him. My daughter experienced a very rough pregnancy, with periodic bleeding and contractions. Her visits to her doctor's office and to the hospital became more frequent as her pregnancy progressed. Yet a heartbeat remained.

The bleeding became severe causing her to grow weaker and weaker. The threat of infection increased, which concerned her doctors. Yet a heartbeat remained.

My daughter lived almost a thousand miles away from me at the time. I began making arrangements to fly out to her after she called and said she didn't think Tyler would make it. In actuality, it became a matter of life and death for my daughter. To say I never considered advising her to end the pregnancy right then would be a lie—I did. The thought of losing *my* child overshadowed all other considerations. Nothing else mattered to me. Yet a heartbeat remained.

When her water broke, I'd already begun packing for my trip. Before she could get to the hospital, Tyler came. The heart beat stopped. He fought to the very end, and I never even knew him.

The grief we felt over the death of Tyler ran deep. We grieved over the fact we could never spend time with him, watch him grow, hear his voice, see his face, hear his laugh or his cry, or watch him play and skin his knees. A life once there, now ended.

In an effort to ease the pain, I put Tyler in a far off section of my mind, closed the door, and turned the key. It seemed easier that way. Maybe it wouldn't hurt so much. There'd be no need to think about him. I now know that wasn't my reason at all. I felt guilt over the thought of advising my daughter to end Tyler's life.

Always a supporter of life, I never considered abortion as an option. Yet when faced with losing my own child, abortion became the *only* option I saw. My daughter thought otherwise. She thought nothing about giving her life for her child. I understood that, but she was *my* child, and I couldn't see giving up her life for anything—not even Tyler.

How God loves us so. He knew, in all His infinite wisdom, I would never be able to live with the loss of my daughter or the abortion of my grandson. So He reached down from heaven and lovingly scooped up this precious little being and brought him home to live with Him amongst the angels.

On those times when I allow my mind to unlock that section where Tyler lives, I usually just sob, because the guilt remains. I must reach for God during those times. He knows my inner most feelings. He tells me each time, "I understand the love of a parent." I guess some day I will accept that.

As the years pass, the hurt weakens. I find I can face Tyler a little more each time.

I consider it reprehensible there are those among us who take the lives of children on a daily, if not hourly, basis. Certainly the topic of abortion is an explosive one. We hear politically correct words used to define a child in the womb and abortion: *embryo, fetus,* and *end a pregnancy* instead of end a life. I'm sure using the term *murder* would be out of the question.

The way I see it, we either believe in a woman's right to have an abortion or we don't. In current language, a person is either pro-life or pro-choice.

The Bible speaks clearly about abortion. It defines life in such a way that there can be no question the writers of the Bible definitely fall on the pro-life side of the debate. The penalties for those who harm babies in utero are pretty serious as stated unquestionably in Exodus 21:22–25. These passages warn that if a baby is harmed through two people fighting, Old Testament law demanded an "eye for an eye, tooth for tooth, hand for hand, foot for foot, burn for burn, wound for wound, bruise for bruise."

Life begins at conception. Scripture tells us life is a precious gift from God—a gift we need to cherish, not seek to destroy. How does one justify the killing of innocent children? Try asking a pro-choice person that question. No matter what comes out of their mouths, it makes no sense to me.

When my grandson died, he had a name, unlike the thousands upon thousands of dead kids with no names. He died from natural causes and not at the hand of an abortionist. We will be judged for whatever stance we take on this issue. Of that I am certain. I'm proud to stand on the side of life.

Tyler never got the chance to form any opinions. Not because my daughter looked in the direction of her *rights*, but rather, she looked in the direction of her child's *life*. Those are the key words. Some might think it's their "right," but in reality, it's the baby's "life."

Tyler never would have survived full term. Neither would my daughter. Her water broke way too soon causing the miscarriage. Too little and not yet at a point where he could make it outside of his mother, Tyler still very much needed her. And though I do ask why, as my grandma used to say, "We will know the answers to our questions by and by."

On the days when I feel emotionally strong, I think of Tyler. I wonder the sort of man he would have been. Would he have been a young gentleman kind and strong? Would he be mischievous like his mother and grandmother? Would he possess a forgiving spirit like his grandfather? Or something else entirely? Considering how Tyler fought to the end, I believe his character would encompass all of those things.

I tend to fret during those times I let myself wonder about

Tyler, and God must bring me back to the place where reason lives. He reminds me of Psalm 139:13–16: "For you created my inmost being; you knit me together in my mother's womb. I praise you because I am fearfully and wonderfully made; your works are wonderful, I know that full well. My frame was not hidden from you when I was made in the secret place, when I was woven together in the depths of the earth. Your eyes saw my unformed body; all the days ordained for me were written in your book before one of them came to be."

As those words flow through my mind, I allow myself to smile, imagining a world with Tyler. I picture him gentle, kind, strong, but, more importantly, safe.

I've never understood the death of a child. I can't get my brain around it. Part of me wants to question God's allowance of such a tragedy. Yet, if not for my faith, the death of my grandson would send me to a padded room. What do those with no faith cling to?

I once knew a woman who lost three of her four children. I stood in awe of her faith. I thought her remarkable. I've known other women with that same kind of courage, and their strength never ceases to amaze me.

Do I wish a different story for Tyler? Sure I do. But when God puts His hand on my heart and guides my mind in a sensible direction, I also realize Tyler left an indelible impression on my life. An impression that allows me to put words to paper and express the sorrow, the guilt, the regret, and even the anger resulting from his loss. That might be a small part of his purpose.

Twenty years since Tyler death and I'm still guarded as to the times I unlock the door to that section of my mind where his memory lives. I do know this—my love for my grandson will never die.

Second Corinthians 4:8–18 can only comfort those who read it as it pertains to trouble and sadness. Paul tells us although we might be pressed on every side, we are not crushed. And even when driven to despair we are never abandoned by God. That's why we should never give up. He explains that our present troubles are small and won't last long. They produce for us a glory that greatly outweighs them and will last forever. The last verse is so powerful: "So we fix our eyes not on what is seen, but on what is unseen, since what is seen is temporary, but what is unseen is eternal."

My daughter now has three children, and they are that extra beat in my heart. On occasion, when I watch them as they sleep or play, I catch a glimpse of Tyler. I see him in that little twinkle in their eyes, the smiles on their faces, the skips in their steps, and the mischief that exudes through every pore in their bodies. How do I know this? I just do. Even though, I never knew Tyler.

CHAPTER SEVEN

What Good Ever Came Out of Being Broke?

LET'S FACE IT, A good portion of the population on earth has experienced or is still experiencing being poor. And there are those in this country, and in other countries, who know the full meaning of poor—a meaning most of us will never really know. But being broke? Well that's another story.

In reality, I know absolutely nothing about being *poor*. I do know what it means to be broke. It's my bet most of us, particularly when we were young and just starting out, know what it means to be broke.

I've been broke most of my life. Being broke simply means you work for your money instead of your money working for you. Many of us know what it's like living paycheck to paycheck. Each month we say to ourselves, "This month I'm going to put a little something away." With each paycheck, we make an effort to start building up our savings account. Well, anyway, we try. Sometimes we succeed. Those are the months we stick out our chests and brag about our accomplishment. We're so proud because an entire two days passed and that little extra money is still there all safe inside the bank. Until something breaks down.

My youngest daughter and her husband bought a house about three years ago. Needless to say they're broke now. They live paycheck to paycheck. After the New Year rolls around, they look forward to doing their income tax return because they know they will get something back, which always helps.

One day she called, frustrated. "Our air conditioner just went out."

I offered my condolences. "Did you call the repairman?"

"Yes."

I could feel her level of aggravation peaking.

"Owning your own home means you get to pay for all the repairs," I said in my mother-knows-best voice.

She was not amused. "We just got our income tax money back, and we were hoping to use it to take a vacation! Now we have to fix the stupid air conditioner!" Her outside voice kicked in.

"Well," I said, "at least you have the money, and it won't put you in a bind. Just be thankful for that."

Silence, silence, silence.

Finally, she said, "I guess you're right, but it doesn't make me feel any better."

That's what being broke is all about. I told her things would get better, they would keep moving forward. Again—silence.

After forty years of marriage, my husband and I don't live paycheck to paycheck anymore, and not because we're wealthy or even financially secure. We just finally see money left over in our account to buy food after we pay our mortgage, cars, and utilities. There's no credit card debt, which makes it even better.

When we began our married life, *nothing* just about summed up our monetary value. My husband didn't even have a job. I did, but it paid very little. We lived in a two-bedroom apartment. After two months of marriage, my husband found work. Things were better, but we remained broke. Between the two of us, our debt was substantial. But we were in love (cue violins), so that made it okay.

I fully believe love is blind, but not in the way that term actually means. Love is blind in that the ones in love are not only blind to each other's faults; they are also blind to everything else around them. Reality never enters into the minds of love-sick fools who think they can live off that love.

Reality found its way into our lives when all of a sudden we found ourselves with three kids. Well, it seemed like all of a sudden. Reality can sneak up on us when we aren't paying attention.

Kids change everything—and not just your love life. They change your bank account too. And they keep changing your bank account until you get them through college and they move out—hopefully for good. We were reassured by friends whose kids were out of the house that they now had more money than they knew what to do with. Seriously? We could expect that in our future? Oh happy day!

Instead, the economy went in the wrong direction. We found ourselves right back at the beginning. Let's think back. What wisdom did I impart to my daughter about things getting better? Oh, and the part about moving forward? Now the sound of silence on the other end of the phone made sense.

Being poor, not just broke, however, brings with it a completely different set of circumstances. What does it mean to be poor? Poor, in the sense you are living its true definition? Meaning you literally possess little or no money or means of support whereby you are dependent on charity. The word impoverished or welfare comes to mind.

Too many human beings live impoverished or poor. We've seen countless documentaries of conditions we couldn't bear our dog living in, conditions people find themselves in every day of their lives. We cry, send money, clothing, food and everything we can think of to help. But it never seems to be enough. The poor are always there.

HIPC is an acronym for "Heavily Indebted Poor Countries." It's a group of countries that experience a high level of poverty and debt overhang. This makes them eligible for special assistance from the International Monetary Fund and the World Bank. Then there are the world's poorest countries. Sorry, but my brain doesn't quite reach out that far. And it's not because I'm not concerned or don't care. I do care. I send what I can to legitimate organizations working on behalf of countries in need. I'm more focused on my own country and do more to help out here. Nonetheless, it's gut-wrenching.

When my girls were young, I used to involve them in giving of their time and talents to others. My husband and I were, at that time in our lives, living paycheck to paycheck, as I mentioned earlier. So giving of our time and talents trumped giving of our dollars and cents.

Santa's Helpers and *Secret Santa* were two things we insisted our girls participate in at Christmas. *Santa's Helpers* worked with the local Children and Family Services office. Families that qualified completed a form that provided information such as number of people in their family, number of adults, ages of children, and gender of children.

All items donated toward the *Santa's Helpers* were housed in a massive warehouse. Inside the warehouse, tables were set in categories: food, clothing, and toys. Local supermarkets, toy stores, clothing stores, etc., donated items for this very special event.

The volunteers were given a form with all the family information on it and a shopping cart. Each of the volunteers then went on a shopping spree throughout the warehouse. My girls loved to volunteer for this event.

At the beginning of their introduction to this worthy cause, they were less than enthusiastic. I found it impossible to tolerate the snobbery that exuded from them. Needless to say, they chose not to argue with my powers of persuasion. I knew once they got involved, they would love it. Giving in this manner never leaves one empty-handed. It fills you to overflowing.

Secret Santa also became a special joy because the girls were allowed to pick out the toy we gave. My kids learned at an early age just how fortunate they were. And although we might have been broke, we certainly weren't poor. In addition to this type of giving, I involved them in other activities where they actually taught others to *fish*. Now that, I must say, is a beautiful sight.

Our town square provided a homeless shelter that sat at the end of the main street. Oh, there were some who made a huge deal about that shelter. Some never wanted it there. They expressed their concerns over the reputation of the town square housing such a facility. The very fact it would draw in so many dirty, homeless, unsightly individuals couldn't be a good thing for the community.

"How about the violence that might occur?" the townspeople lamented.

"What if something happens and it appears on the local, state, or national news?" they all said. "How will it look?"

The talk went on and on and on, ad nauseam. The homeless shelter stayed in business for years with never an incident, never any violence, and never any embarrassing news—local, state or otherwise. There were lots of dirty, homeless, and unsightly individuals, to be sure. I volunteered there at least once a month. I loved every minute of it.

At the beginning, I came across as an idiot. I knew nothing about dealing with the homeless. The man who ran the shelter was a saint—a true gift from God. He possessed the patience of Job, and I'm not talking about patience with the homeless people. I'm talking about patience with the volunteers, because we were all idiots at the beginning.

The first time my husband and I showed up, we came with high hopes and a plan to change all of humanity right along with this disease known as homelessness. John (appropriate name), the guy who ran the shelter, saw thousands of our kind pass through his door. He just smiled when we got there that night. We immediately noticed three families, each with small children. They all lived out of their cars. Along with the families, there looked to be forty other people—all men.

When my husband saw those kids, he ran to the nearest Wal-Mart and bought toys, snacks, and sodas. He went home and popped enough popcorn to feed the entire town. We were both so proud. Again, John just smiled and watched as we proceeded to self-destruct.

The shelter ran like this: The people checked in at the front desk. The clerk there confiscated any contraband such as booze, drugs, or weapons. They didn't get those back, either. That was the price they paid for bringing the stuff into the facility in the first place. The shelter allowed them a shower. The volunteers washed their clothes. They received dinner and could either watch TV or read until lights out at 11:00 p.m. Rise and shine came at 6:00 a.m. When they got up, they found their clothing washed, dried, folded, and lying neatly on a table. They received breakfast before they left the shelter.

After dinner on our first volunteer night, my husband and I proudly laid out all the wonderful toys, snacks, sodas, and popcorn we purchased. We stood back with big smiles on our faces, proud to be us. But not one toy left that table—not one snack, soda, or piece of popcorn consumed. Our big smiles faded. We became confused and angry. We came there to help these people, for goodness sake. John just smiled, put his arms around us, and walked us into his office. I'll never forget as long as I live what he said.

"I do so appreciate all the efforts you both made to bring what you thought would be well received. But let me explain something to you that I know you don't know. It's not that they don't appreciate your gesture. It's that if they allow themselves to indulge in all of these wonderful things tonight, tomorrow, when they don't have them, will be much harder. They know they can't get those things on their own right now, so it's easier not to have them at all. It makes tomorrow easier to bear."

It made perfect sense. Words cannot express how stupid we felt. John saw our embarrassment. The kindness he showed in helping us to understand we weren't alone in our wanting to give in that manner helped us to realize that giving of ourselves far exceeded the giving of stuff. I carry that with me still.

The people we met in that shelter were no different from ourselves. Some fell on hard times. Some didn't want any better. Some fought addictions and mental conditions. Overall, they were simply human beings who needed to know someone cared. Believe me, we are all just a breath away from being in that same situation. Circumstances can turn on a dime, and we can find ourselves in a position we never thought we would ever be in. That is a fact. I saw it in the faces of those I served.

We eventually grew in our knowledge and vowed never to make that kind of mistake again. We still made mistakes, but we realized how blessed and honored we felt knowing, serving, and giving of ourselves to those who passed through the doors of that special place.

The Bible speaks often and clearly about the poor. In Acts 20:35 we read: "In everything I did, I showed you that by this kind of hard work we must help the weak, remembering the words the Lord Jesus himself said: 'It is more blessed to give than to receive.'"

In Hebrews 13:16 we read: "And do not forget to do good and to share with others, for with such sacrifices God is pleased." Then in Luke 12:33–34: "Sell your possessions and give to the poor. Provide purses for yourselves that will not wear out, a treasure in heaven that will never fail, where no thief comes near and no moth destroys. For where your treasure is, there your heart will be also." Our instructions continue as seen in Proverbs 22:16: "One who oppresses the poor to increase his wealth and one who gives gifts to the rich—both come to poverty."

My favorite passage speaks to the very heart of giving and receiving. It's found in Luke 14:12–14: "Then Jesus said to his host, 'When you give a luncheon or dinner, do not invite your friends, your brothers or sisters, your relatives, or your rich neighbors; if you do, they may invite you back and so you will be repaid. But when you give a banquet, invite the poor, the crippled, the lame, the blind, and you will be blessed. Although they cannot repay you, you will be repaid at the resurrection of the righteous.'" Clearly, the Bible says much regarding the poor and giving.

In our younger days, we are all about making that money. We want a better life for ourselves. That includes a house, car, and all the things we can hoard. We can't wait to say we've arrived. We ain't broke anymore, honey!

We work our entire lives to get to that point whereby we can sit back, relax, and enjoy the fruits of our labors. Unfortunately for many of us who thought we were almost there—the baby boomers in particular—the bottom fell out of the economy not so long ago, and our once big, fat, lovely 401K's went back to the point when we first started investing in them. Our dreams of a nice comfortable retirement vanished. Some of us either lost our jobs, lost our shirts in the stock market, or lost our minds. Some of us don't know from one day to the next if we'll even have a job. Tightening our belts became an American pastime. Especially at Christmas.

It's a vicious circle. When there's no consumption, we die. Retailers saw record low spending at that time. My family spent less than in previous years. We skipped the family tradition of drawing names. We held our breath waiting to see if any of us lost our job when the New Year rolled around.

It's funny, but in times of need, God designed us to think. We do that *thinking outside-the-box thing*. One Christmas my daughter and her husband made us Christmas tree ornaments out of homemade dough. They shaped each one by hand, baked them in the oven, hand painted them, put each of our names on them, wrapped them in bags from at least ten Christmases ago, and proudly presented them to us Christmas morning. They are priceless. If the richest man in the world offered me all he possessed for those precious little ornaments, I would tell him to hit the road. Those adorable, love-filled little gems highlighted our Christmas. If my house burned down today, I would grab them first.

We spend our days, our nights, and our lives working for or fretting over money. In actuality, the best times of our lives are probably when we're the most broke.

I remember at the beginning of our marriage, the bills seemed never ending. Something always broke down when money seemed out of reach. The ironic thing is, we laughed more as a family. We gave of ourselves more often. We used our imaginations more.

Many of us find ourselves going through that period in our lives when being broke seems as though it will be our life's story. That saying about necessity being the mother of invention is true. Although being broke sucks the majority of the time, a lot of good can actually come out of being broke. Our appreciation for what we *do* possess is one of those things.

My grandfather used to say, "We should be grateful for what we have and not fret over what we don't." I don't ever remember him fretting over the things he didn't have. And you know what? He lived a really long time. So, what good ever came out of being broke? You figure it out.

CHAPTER EIGHT

Things Our Mothers Used to Tell Us

R EMEMBER ALL THE STUFF our mothers used to tell us? Stuff like don't have sex, don't do drugs or I'll kill you, and turn down that awful sounding rock 'n roll? In short—sex, drugs, and rock 'n roll. There must be some kind of manual all mothers read and then repeat back to their kids. I offer that up as if I'm not a mother, although I am. I certainly don't remember reading any manual but I still said all the same harebrained stuff to my kids that my mother said to me. You know—stuff like don't have sex, don't do drugs or I'll kill you, and turn down that awful sounding rock 'n roll!

In my day, mothers tended to over-exaggerate the sex thing in an effort to scare their daughters to death. For example, my mother told me once that if I put my legs over a boy's lap I could get pregnant. The visual of that boggles my brain. I think she stretched the truth a wee bit. Certainly that action could lead to other things, which could ultimately lead to pregnancy. But I'm rather certain the actual act of sex would be less likely to happen while sitting in the den with your parents watching every move you made. Did tactics like this work? Absolutely! Our mothers put forth an extreme effort to ensure the end result—getting us to do what they wanted us to do.

In my mother's house, the subject of drugs was a non-issue. Her point-of-view remained consistent. "If you do drugs, you won't have to worry about a drug killing you. I'll kill you." It made perfect sense to her. My mother put the fear of drug abuse in me so as not to leave room for any misunderstanding. I envisioned people on drugs flying out of windows, jumping off bridges or walking stark naked into traffic. Fortunately for me, I actually heeded her words. It probably saved my life. Especially since drugs were everywhere in the sixties.

Rock 'n Roll ran high on my mother's hit list of "don't even think about it." She secretly wanted to wipe that music from the airwaves. Mother even referred to a specific list of artists she forbade me to listen to. Any attempt on my part to listen to their songs would be met with a blowback I would not soon forget. "Pure garbage, made up by a bunch of acid heads," my mother's words rang out. And with that, the music industry ushered in "Acid Rock." My poor mother's head exploded at that point.

We all knew the song "Louie Louie" contained the forbidden "F" bomb in it (totally untrue), and when the song "Strawberry Fields Forever" was played backwards it said, "Paul is dead," (another myth). She also believed it possible the record might even say "God is dead." Nope, not that either. Both were silly rumors gone berserk. The experts (who were those people anyway?) provided her with this information. Of course my mother never allowed me to listen to those songs anyway.

Sex, drugs, and rock 'n roll are often the teenage issues mothers take on. But when we're small, our mothers tell us other things that don't make any sense whatsoever. They are intended as shock value. This list might bring back a few memories:

1. Don't climb on anything, or you'll fall and break your neck.
   So now I have a fear of heights. Thanks, Mom!
2. If you tell a lie, you'll get a sore on your tongue.
   Seriously?
3. If you listen to loud music, you'll go deaf.
   What? I can't hear you.
4. If you pick your nose and stick your finger up too far, you'll poke your brain.
   That's impossible. Kids don't have brains.
5. If you swallow a watermelon seed, a gigantic watermelon will grow in your stomach.

Did they really think we'd believe that?
6. If you eat dirt (some kids actually do this), a tree will grow in your stomach and then you'll get worms.
   Okay—so I ate dirt. No trees or worms are now nor have they ever been in my stomach.
7. If you pop your knuckles, you'll make them bigger.
   Is there medical backup to support this claim?
8. If you bite your fingernails and swallow them, a giant fingernail will grow in your stomach.
   What is it with things growing in your stomach?
9. If you blow in a baby's mouth, his eyes will pop out.
   That's just plain sick.
10. If you stick your tongue out and touch your nose, your ears will grow to the size of a donkey's ears.
    Wait a minute. Is that what happened to that kid in my third grade class?
11. You should always wear clean underwear in case you're in an accident.
    You are going to have soiled underwear if you're in an accident.
12. A woman's reputation is like fine china. Once it's broken, it can never be repaired.
    Gotta agree with that one.
13. There are starving kids in China who would love to eat that food on your plate.
    Just another one of those scare tactics. I always thought even starving kids wouldn't eat the stuff my mom wanted me to eat.
14. You'll sit at this table and clean your plate if it takes you until the cows come home.
    Until the cows do what? We never even owned any cows.
15. You act like you were jerked up instead of raised.
    Being jerked up would hurt—right?

16. Do you think I'm talking just to hear myself talk?
    I actually answered that question once. I don't remember what happened after that.
17. Wait until your father comes home. He'll knock you into tomorrow morning.
    I waited. He did.
18. Shut your mouth and answer me when I ask you a question.
    Unless you are a professional ventriloquist, that's just physically impossible.
19. I hope and pray that when you grow up and have children, they act just like you.
    That's a curse. And it actually works!
20. If your grandmother could see how you're acting, she would turn over in her grave.
    Can you do that when you're dead?
21. Just keep crying, and I'll give you something to cry about.
    That makes no sense at all.
22. Because I said so, that's why; so don't ask again.
    My favorite and I've used it many times.

We all would be afflicted with every single one of these plagues if our mothers had anything to do with it.

Following true-to-form, my poor children listened to all this ridiculous rhetoric passed down from generation to generation. My grandchildren now listen to it from their mother, my daughter. It's like some kind of hideous disease from which none of us can escape.

I can remember being in awe as this craziness came falling out of my mouth. My children gave me the same blank stare I gave my mother when she spewed this jargon at me.

Even though we can intellectually pick apart every single one of these sayings, I conclude that one of the reasons our mothers tell us all this nonsense is because it's their way of telling us how very much they love us. We, in turn, take up the cause and dump it right back on our own kids, whom we love just as much.

As a child I remember thinking my mother yelled at me an awful lot. My daddy never yelled. Being a drill sergeant in the Army, he never needed to. Enough said. Plus, I found it more fun to agitate my mother just to hear her yell. When I became a bit older, I asked my daddy why my mother always yelled. He said, "Parents yell when they think their child has drifted too far away to hear them." I know now it's simply fear.

As parents—as mothers—our biggest fear is that our children will drift too far away to hear us. I'm willing to bet the majority of mothers out there yelled at their kids at one time or another. I know I did. I'm quite sure all the TV doctors would have a field day with that, but let me state right now—and very clearly—I do not care! There are more mothers in the world who genuinely love their children than there are those who don't. Yelling comes with the job.

My mother and I didn't get along much during my growing up years, but I always knew one thing—she loved me. If the yelling ever stopped, there'd be something to worry about because that meant she no longer cared.

After all these years, I look back on my relationship with my mother and my relationship with my own children and I realize there really wasn't as much yelling going on as I imagined. It just seemed at the time as if that's all we did. Through the eyes and mind of an adult, I know many times I deserved that yelling. Other times, I now realize, my mother didn't yell, she just said all those crazy things.

The Bible makes some very strong statements as to our

responsibilities as mothers and, yes, as children. As it pertains to mothers, Proverbs 23:12–16 tells us: "Apply your heart to instruction and your ears to words of knowledge. Do not withhold discipline from a child; if you punish them with the rod, they will not die. Punish them with the rod and save them from death. My son, if your heart is wise, then my heart will be glad indeed; my inmost being will rejoice when your lips speak what is right."

A good mother knows she must discipline her children in order to experience the delight that comes from knowing the things that come out of her children's mouths are right and good and just. This is every mother's wish. As mothers, we sigh in relief and thanksgiving when we know we raised young men and women who go on to make a difference, either in the world or in the lives of others.

We all believe this verse in Psalm 127:3: "Children are a heritage from the Lord, offspring a reward from him." Our children are truly a gift to be cherished.

The Bible doesn't leave out instructions for children. We read in Proverbs 1:8: "Listen, my son, to your father's instruction and do not forsake your mother's teaching." Proverbs 30:17 tells us: "The eye that mocks a father, that scorns an aged mother, will be pecked out by the ravens of the valley, will be eaten by the vultures." And again in Proverbs 20:20 we read: "If someone curses their father or mother, their lamp will be snuffed out in pitch darkness." Finally, Exodus 21:17: "Anyone who curses their father or mother is to be put to death." But wait. Proverbs 15:20 and Leviticus 19:3 also provide warnings to children in the treatment of their mothers.

Wow, that's some strong instructions geared toward children, young and old alike. We can't deny that the Bible makes clear children bear a great responsibility to their mothers, the ones who care for them, love them and teach them. Their responsibility is to show respect for those incredible women who gave them life.

Likewise, mothers should continue to love their children with the unconditional love only a mother can give.

When my girls get together they go nuts. They sit around looking at old pictures and laughing about the way they say I made them dress. This is a total lie because they liked the stuff they wore. We never seem to agree on the things that happened in our house during their growing up years. They tell "Mom stories" that causes their sides to hurt and tears to roll down their faces from all the laughter. But those years with our mothers are probably the best times of our lives. We just don't seem to believe that while we're listening to the things our mothers used to tell us.

CHAPTER NINE

I Never Did Like Dogs Anyway

A FAMILY, COUPLE, OR individual takes on great responsibilities when they decide to adopt pets. Sometimes it becomes a love-hate relationship. Remember the movie, *Beethoven*? I love that movie. It not only shows the lovey-dovey, isn't-that-cute part of having a pet, it also shows the reality of having a pet. For the record, in the movie, I found myself on the dad's side the majority of the time—especially when Beethoven ransacked the house. That's why our dog was an outside dog.

The catch is we never quite manage not falling in love with our pets. For all the destruction they cause, the times they either pee or poop on the floor, the money spent on food, vet visits, and obedience schools, the aggravation—they are just too cute for words, no matter how ugly some of them might be. Eventually, they become a part of the family.

Buckus was our family's dog. A ninety-pound, solid-white, German shepherd—known as a white shepherd. We all loved him to pieces. Undoubtedly the best dog I've ever owned. That's saying something because I grew up with and owned many dogs before Buckus. White shepherds are one of the best breeds a family could own. They're loyal, friendly, watchful, smart, and very protective. Buckus possessed all of these qualities.

Some believe white shepherds should not be recognized as a legitimate breed, that being white disqualifies them from participating in local dog shows or even the coveted *Best in Show*. They see their whiteness as a defect.

In the end, I certainly didn't care if any organization ever recognized my dog. I recognized him, my family recognized him, and that's it—good enough for me! Buckus was beautiful, we loved him, and he will always be a part of our family.

We didn't know a thing about white shepherds when we got

Buckus as a pup. A friend's uncle owned Buckus, but the uncle became ill and could no longer care for the dog. Our friend asked if we would like to adopt Buckus.

We told her we would need to think about it and talk it over with our three children. At the time, our kids were thirteen, six, and three—all girls. Our oldest never met an animal she didn't like. Our middle one hated anything not human. Our youngest fell in between the two.

So we presented the offer to the girls at the dinner table one night. Of course our oldest screamed, "Yes, yes, yes!"

The youngest just grinned. "I don't know."

The middle one ran out of the room. After bulldozing down the bedroom door (she evidently nailed it shut) and promising to buy her a toy store, we decided four to one to accept the offer. We became a family of two parents, three kids, and one dog. What had we gotten ourselves into?

We spent the week before we brought Buckus home getting ready for him. We bought a dog house, built a pen, and put up a runner. We bought dog food, dog treats, bowls for food and water. And, yes, a dog toothbrush.

Our youngest wanted to hang pink and purple curtains in the dog house. The oldest wanted to know if the dog could sleep in her room at night. The middle one wanted to run away from home. It was a happy time.

When we brought our new dog into the house, he immediately peed on the floor. Our oldest laughed and laughed. The youngest hid behind the oldest not wanting any of the pee to get on her shoes. The middle one ran out of the room and barricaded herself in her bedroom again. It was a happy time.

After we calmed the dog down, got him outside and acquainted with his new house and new surroundings, we decided he needed a name. The oldest wanted to name him Snowball.

The youngest giggled and said, "I don't know."

The middle one yelled down from her barricaded bedroom, "Get that thing out of the house!" My husband and I didn't like any of those suggestions. It was a happy time.

Finally, my husband said, "I'm naming the dog. I live with four females. This is the only other male in the house. I'm naming the dog."

The oldest rolled her eyes, because that's what thirteen-year-olds do.

The youngest grinned and said, "Daddy loves doggie."

The middle one yelled down from her barricaded bedroom, "Did you get that thing out of the house yet?" It was a happy time.

Being the only sane adult in the room, I agreed my husband should name the dog.

Somewhere, I'm sure of it, I heard the sound of a drum roll. My husband stuck out his chest and proclaimed, "His name will be Buckus!"

We all stared at him. You know, the way women look at men when they've said something stupid.

The oldest said, "Who names their dog Buckus?"

My husband smiled. "Rocky Balboa, that's who!" It really didn't matter to him if the girls knew who Rocky Balboa was or not. It only mattered that my husband knew.

The youngest clapped her hands. "I like Buckus!"

The middle one yelled down from her barricaded bedroom, "That's a stupid name! I'm going to go live with Papa and Granny!"

Yes, indeed, it was a happy time.

As I look back on that day, I now realize it marked the beginning of many happy years our family would spend with Buckus.

We soon learned that Buckus ate—a lot! In fact, he ate anything not nailed down. He also liked to dig. And dig, and dig. By the time he turned three years old, he dug a complete tunnel under his house—truly quite sophisticated. According to rumors, he stashed at least a year's supply of bones in that tunnel.

It didn't take long for the girls to fall in love with Buckus. Yes, even the middle one. Every time one of them went outside, Buckus stood right there with them keeping them safe. Of course, others thought Buckus was a wolf or some sort of vicious animal like that due to his size and color. But, those who got to know him loved him. We discovered if we introduced a new face to Buckus, that person immediately became his friend forever. If we failed to make that introduction—look out! Buckus appointed himself the protector of our yard, our house, and our kids. We couldn't have asked for a better dog.

When we moved from our home in Atlanta, Georgia, we couldn't imagine how Buckus would adjust to our new city in Texas. The landscape didn't look at all like Georgia. We found the weather, especially the humidity, between the two cities quite different. Plus all of Buckus' friends and other family members weren't in Texas. It was not a happy time.

We decided my parents would keep Buckus until we settled into our new house. My husband wanted to build a doghouse for Buckus instead of buying one. It took him a week to build that house. He installed a little swirly fan on top of the roof to keep the inside of the house cool. Next he equipped it with running water that came on when the sprinklers came on to keep Buckus' water bucket full. It was truly magnificent.

When the time arrived for Buckus to see his new home, my father and brother-in-law took him to the airport. Eight months had passed since we said good-bye and left him with my parents. Excited, we arrived at the airport an hour early. As they brought

Buckus into the terminal, the celebration began. I'm sure it looked like some sort of family reunion. As insane as it sounds, our family included Buckus.

Buckus settled right in as if he'd lived in Texas his entire life—all that worrying for nothing. He loved the pool, especially during August, which is the hottest month of the year in Texas. On those scorching days, Buckus would park his behind on the top step of the pool and sit there for hours.

Buckus' new surroundings didn't stop him from digging, however. This unexplored territory made way for more places to bury bones. My husband scolded Buckus just like one of our kids. He would look at Buckus with a stern face and say, "Buckus, have you been digging?" Buckus would run lickety-split and get as far back into his house as possible, so my husband couldn't see him.

One day my husband went outside and saw Buckus in the bushes, digging away. He yelled, "Buckus are you digging?"

Buckus saw my husband standing not more than two feet away from his digging spot and knew he couldn't run fast enough to get to his house without being caught. My husband laughed as Buckus came creeping out from behind the bushes. He crawled over to the fence and slowly started to sneak down the side of it. Yep, he was invisible! Or so he thought. That silly dog actually believed if he crept slowly enough, he wouldn't be seen. Fortunately for Buckus, my husband couldn't stop laughing and couldn't bring himself to punish him.

We hold dear many funny Buckus stories, and now that Buckus is gone, it makes us smile to think of them. Nine to twelve years is the average lifespan for a shepherd. Buckus lived sixteen years.

About two months before Buckus' death, his hip dysplasia became severe. He couldn't walk any longer. He could only drag his hind legs. We took him to the vet. My husband told her if she couldn't do anything for him, we wanted her to put him down. The girls were hysterical, but we had no choice. We couldn't allow him to suffer any longer.

The vet said she wanted to try something, and if it didn't work, she would put him down. She called us the next day. "Come get your dog. He's chasing my ostriches all over the yard!"

The celebration began! The girls cried. We cried. We rushed to the vet to get Buckus and bring him home.

Two months passed and Buckus seemed as happy and healthy as ever. Little did we know on this particular day, we'd be saying our good-byes.

My husband and I got ready for work on an unusually hot July day. By this time, only our middle and youngest still lived at home. We told the girls to make sure Buckus got plenty of water all day and to let him get in the pool as much as he wanted. We even told them to hose him off every now and then if he didn't want to get in the pool.

As I started to leave, for some strange reason I stopped in front of the kitchen window. Buckus sat proudly outside of his dog house. I stood there, just looking at him. In return, he looked back at me, tilted his head as if to say, "It's okay. You can go. I'm going to be just fine." In all of our years with Buckus, I'd never done that. I went on to work with a peculiar feeling in my gut.

That afternoon, my middle daughter (yes, the one who wanted nothing to do with the dog and wanted to leave home) called, screaming in the phone, "Mom, Mom, Buckus is dead! Buckus is dead!"

As my mind flashed back to the morning, I realized Buckus took that time to say good-bye to me. I began to cry. I called my husband but could barely get the words out. I didn't need to—he knew. When we arrived home, we discovered our daughter was right. I guess a part of both of us hoped she might be wrong.

As we all stood around Buckus, the reality of his death started to sink in.

"The strangest thing happened this morning," my husband said. "As I was leaving for work, I decided to walk out to Buckus' pen and tell him good-bye. I usually just yell out the back door, 'see ya later, big guy.' When I came outside, Buckus was just sitting here with what seemed to be the biggest smile on his face. I patted him on the head, and he licked my hand. I didn't want to leave, but he looked right at me as if he were telling me everything was going to be fine and he was going to be okay."

I looked at my husband and burst into tears again. It would be a few days before I told my family about that morning when I looked out the kitchen window.

We carefully wrapped Buckus in sheets, called the vet and took him to her office. She offered the names of pet cemeteries, etc. My husband decided he didn't want Buckus away from the family in a pet cemetery. He said if we buried him in the back yard, we would never want to sell our house, which might become a problem later on down the road. Finally, he decided to cremate Buckus. His ashes, carefully placed in a beautiful wooden case, rest safely inside our home to this day.

When Buckus died, we all mourned his death for quite a while. We still get a bit choked up when we talk about him, because we miss him. He protected and played with our girls during most of their growing-up years. He was the best thing that ever happened to our middle daughter as she is now only afraid of bugs. We will always miss him.

I've not found a lot of scripture that speaks to things like animals going to heaven, whether animals do or do not have souls, animal rights or animal cruelty; therefore, I don't feel equipped to speak to that. I'm not a theologian, but I do feel that God holds animals dear to His heart. Evidence of that appears in Luke 12:6 where we read: "Are not five sparrows sold for two pennies? Yet not one of them is forgotten by God."

God expects us to care for our animals and to allow our animals to rest and eat. Proverbs 27:23 reads: "Be sure you know the condition of your flocks, give careful attention to your herds . . ."

In particular, Job 12:7–10 does speak to animals, mankind, and the Creator: "But ask the animals, and they will teach you, or the birds in the sky, and they will tell you; or speak to the earth, and it will teach you, or let the fish in the sea inform you. Which of all these does not know that the hand of the Lord has done this? In his hand is the life of every creature and the breath of all mankind."

Personally, I believe my family will see Buckus again. But that's just my quirky side coming out.

My youngest child is now all grown up and married—with a dog! Buddy is his name and destruction is his game. This dog jumps higher and moves faster than any dog I ever saw in my life. He loves tissues. He loves to chew them up and tear them into shreds. He can find a tissue anywhere, and it doesn't even matter if the tissue is hiding beneath ten thousand pounds of whatever. Don't even think of putting a tissue in your pocket. He can smell it out, wait till you're not paying attention, then run, jump, and grab that tissue right out of your pocket, and you'll never know what hit you.

He drives me crazy sometimes. No, he drives me crazy most of the time. But, and here's the kicker, I love him. He got sick; I cried. It turned serious; I cried. He could have died; I cried harder. This dog isn't even my dog, and I'm attached to him. It's crazy.

All in all, dogs are the best. I personally will never own another one. It's just too much emotion. But I figure it really doesn't matter because I never did like dogs anyway.

CHAPTER TEN

Miss Fields Was a Tough Old Bird

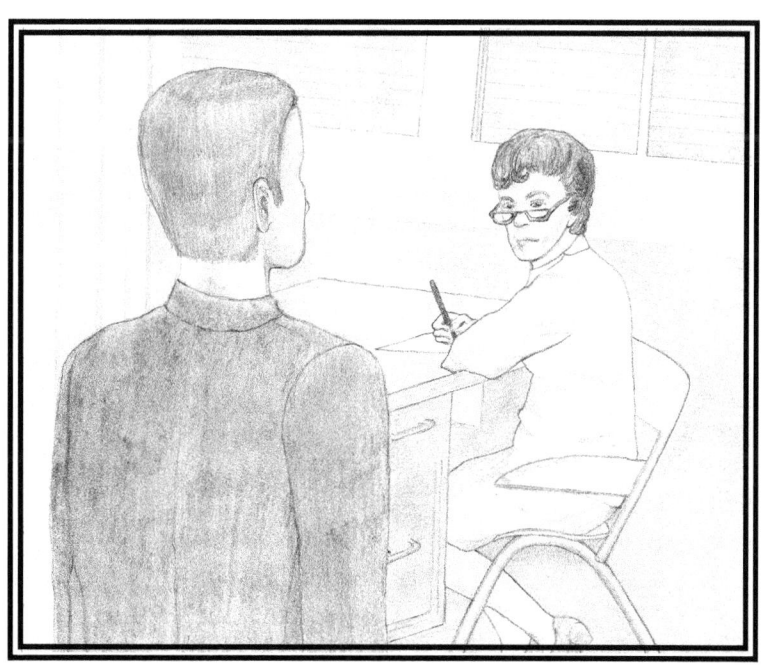

COULD THERE BE ANYTHING harder than senior English? I think not. History ran a close second, but senior English took the gold in the category of difficulty. Lucky for me, Miss Onice Fields happened to be my high school senior English teacher. From my high school yearbook I know that she was a B.A. graduate of Peabody College and a M.A. graduate of Vanderbilt University.

But I never knew anything else about Miss Fields other than she was the hardest teacher who ever taught at my high school. Plus, she taught senior English. Those two things produced a deadly combination. Added together, they spelled O-M-G! Translated it meant *Oh My Grades!* Why? Because the majority of students walked away from that class with a C, D, or F.

Everyone knew if they didn't pass senior English, they wouldn't graduate, so getting Miss Fields as your teacher could be a kid's worst nightmare. Here's where that "however" word comes into play. However, *everybody* wanted Miss Fields for senior English. Were we out of our minds or what? No, we knew that having Miss Fields as a teacher typically turned out to be the best thing that could happen to a student. Not only did she earn the title "hardest teacher," she also earned the title "best teacher," which often goes together.

I loved having Miss Fields as my senior English teacher—and not just because of this super cute guy in my class, either. When I walked into that classroom, the world of English literature came to life.

Every single day Miss Fields wrote a "Thought for the Day" on the chalkboard. Funny the things one remembers after forty plus years. We looked forward to seeing what that thought would be. I never knew where she got those "thoughts." I always figured she just made them up. There were no computers back then, so she couldn't just look up "thought for the day" and choose from a million or so results. Most likely she got them from a book. A what? Yes, a book. When I think back over the ones I remember, I realize some were definitely famous quotes. I'm quite sure others came out of her head.

But it never mattered where she got them. The anticipation of them made us want to come to class. Pretty smart lady, I'd say. Once we were in her classroom, we were hers, and she filled our heads and our hearts with the world of English literature.

We all knew Miss Onice Fields to be a Christian woman. How did we know? She told us so. Gasp! How about that for being bold before being bold was cool? She shared her beliefs with us, and, in turn, we shared our beliefs with her. We were never told that conversations about religion were a bad thing. We never heard about students and teachers not being allowed to speak of what they believed in school. If such a rule ever existed, we certainly didn't obey it.

Miss Fields' primary rule when sharing our beliefs or thoughts: respect each other's opinions or leave the class permanently. Ask me how many left the class. Zero. We knew she meant it. None of us wanted to chance being kicked out. So every day after we completed our lesson, Miss Fields allowed an at-will discussion about anything we wanted to talk about.

One day, and I remember this vividly, Miss Fields shared with us the story of a former student. The story went like this: Being a devout atheist at the ripe old age of seventeen, this student believed beyond a shadow of a doubt that no God existed. He based his belief, I'm sure, on his vast years of experience and knowledge.

On one particular day, he and Miss Fields got into a conversation about her faith, his lack of faith, and life after death.

"What if you're wrong?" she asked.

"So, what if you're wrong?" An intelligent reply, right?

Miss Fields just smiled. "Let's look at that. According to your theory, if I'm wrong, nothing will happen. I will die a stupid old woman who was duped her entire life by the fantasy of a God that did not exist. And that's okay, because this stupid old woman has been happy her entire, duped life. However if you're wrong, well, let's just say I wouldn't want to be you."

The kid got mad and walked out. After that, she said, their relationship went downhill. He graduated, and she thought she would never see him again. Then one day, a few years later, while sitting at her desk in her classroom after school, there came a knock on the half opened door. She looked up. In the doorway stood a very nice looking young man decked out in a suit.

"May I help you?" she asked.

"It's great to see you, Miss Fields."

She couldn't place the young man's face. "I'm so sorry, but do I know you?"

"You do indeed. I was one of your students, once upon a time. We had a very interesting conversation about your faith, life after death, and my non-belief in God. You asked me a question."

"What if you're wrong?" Miss Fields smiled.

They both laughed. Miss Fields walked over to the nice looking young man and held out her hand. He patted it gently, and then they embraced as long lost friends.

"You made me so mad that day, Miss Fields."

"Yes, I know."

"I thought about what you said for a long, long time. It drove me crazy. When I found out you were still here, I had to come see you."

"I'm so glad you did."

"I wanted you to know what that conversation, and the

question you asked, meant in my life. I became a Christian over a year ago, and now I'm attending seminary because God has called me to ask others—'What if you're wrong?'"

Miss Fields said she never cried so much in her life. Looking around the classroom that day, I'm sure we all felt the same.

Teaching a bunch of teenagers how to listen to another person is not an easy task. Miss Fields did it with ease. As we learned the art of listening, we also learned the wonders of English literature. Shakespeare made more sense. Poems made more sense. Even *Of Mice and Men* stimulated conversation. That little classroom became a hotbed of debated ideas.

This woman's ability to captivate an audience of overactive teenagers is something I can't explain. Yet not only did she possess the ability to captivate, she possessed the ability to connect. That's a gift.

Up and coming teachers don't learn that in college or during student teaching.

I decided to do a bit of research on what it actually means to be a teacher. The dictionary's definitions left me unsatisfied.

Then I turned to the Bible and found Deuteronomy 6:6–9: "These commandments that I give you today are to be on your hearts. Impress them on your children. Talk about them when you sit at home and when you walk along the road, when you lie down and when you get up. Tie them as symbols on your hands and bind them on your foreheads. Write them on the doorframes of your houses and on your gates." (Impress here means teach.) I see Miss Fields in this scripture as she talked with us during every part of the day, whether we were sitting together in the classroom or other places, because her words stayed with us.

Next Proverbs 22:6 tells us: "Start children off on the way they should go, and even when they are old they will not turn from it."

(Start here means train/teach.) Miss Fields appears here also as, even now, in my adult years, I remember the things she taught me. And then in Titus 2:7–8 we read: "In everything set them an example by doing what is good. In your teaching show integrity, seriousness and soundness of speech that cannot be condemned, so that those who oppose you may be ashamed because they have nothing bad to say about us." I see her here as she stood for all we looked up to and admired.

Of course as a kid I always loved the verse in Ephesians 6:4: "Fathers, do not exasperate your children; instead, bring them up in the training and instruction of the Lord." Miss Fields never exasperated us but instead taught us and gave us a thirst for learning.

Jesus is known as the greatest teacher who ever lived. Mark 10:13–16 tells us: "People were bringing little children to Jesus for him to place his hands on them, but the disciples rebuked them. When Jesus saw this, he was indignant. He said to them, 'Let the little children come to me, and do not hinder them, for the kingdom of God belongs to such as these. Truly I tell you, anyone who will not receive the kingdom of God like a little child will never enter it.' And he took the children in his arms, placed his hands on them and blessed them." Once again Miss Fields appears. She never grew tired of teaching. She celebrated when we got it and delighted in our learning.

Now those definitions satisfied me better.

It occurred to me after I read them that the dictionary merely defines the word teacher. The Bible defines the essence of a teacher. The dictionary speaks to the word teacher as something that is done, where the Bible speaks to the word teacher as that which one is. Miss Fields didn't typify the dictionary-defined teacher. She exemplified the Biblically defined teacher.

Never let it be said Miss Fields came across as anything less than a disciplinarian. That's a lost word—disciplinarian. I wonder how many remember what it means. Regardless of definitions, we all knew Miss Fields as a disciplinarian. Guess what? I never heard anyone complain. When we walked through that classroom door, we knew better than to test her. Believe me, you wouldn't win. She expected obedience, and we were obedient—at least in her classroom.

It's a funny thing about expectations. Miss Fields *expected* that we would come to love English literature as she did. She *expected* us to respect each other and our different points of view and that we would never tire of learning. She *expected* us to stand up for our beliefs and stand against the things we knew were wrong. Her expectations were that we would grow into responsible adults. I'm betting we all lived up to Miss Fields' expectations.

Sitting in the classroom of a true teacher is a wonderful experience. If you gathered a large group of people together and asked, "Who remembers the name of the best teacher you ever had in school?" I'd be willing to bet every hand would go up. Wouldn't it be a treat to be able to contact that teacher and honor him or her by saying, "Thank you?"

Being a teacher is unappreciated and underpaid. True teachers, however, don't really care about that. They just want to teach. In my family, there are at least eleven teachers. I so admire them all. It's not an easy profession. Miss Fields just made it look easy.

Today, teaching is harder than when Miss Fields taught. But I don't think it's all because of the kids. I think it's because of the system and the manner in which it's run. We took out of our schools everything that once made them great. We made it difficult for our teachers to teach because we're afraid, and in turn our teachers are afraid. They're afraid of losing their job, of offending someone, of standing up for themselves, or anything else for that matter.

Although Miss Fields' senior English class was my hardest class in high school, I don't regret a single day I sat in that room. Miss Fields never feared teaching or offending, if need be. She never shied away from sharing her faith. She never ran away from discipline. She had no fear in her expectations of her students. She demanded our best. Simply put—she was not afraid to be a teacher.

Every school in our nation needs at least one Miss Fields. I'll never forget her or the lessons she taught me. I know I'm the better for having her in my life at a time when I needed her kind of strength. We all adored her. Just ask any of her students. They'll all tell you the same thing. Miss Fields was a tough old bird!

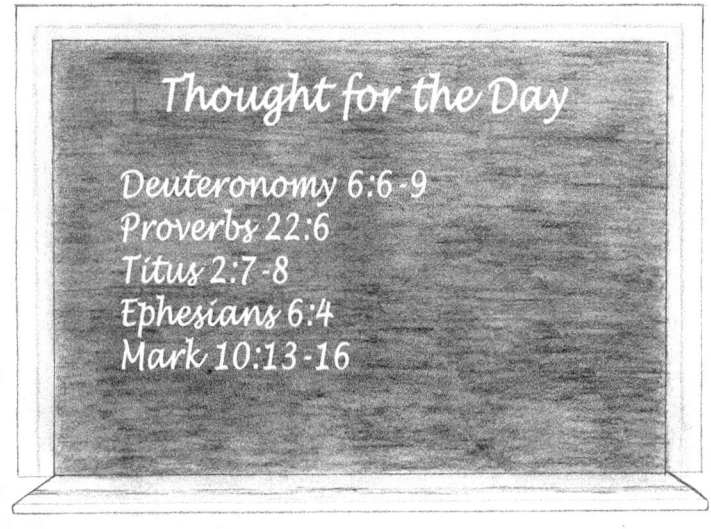

Thought for the Day

Deuteronomy 6:6-9
Proverbs 22:6
Titus 2:7-8
Ephesians 6:4
Mark 10:13-16

CHAPTER ELEVEN

Skye for President

IT'S A KNOWN FACT that when you ask a kid a question about anything, you'd better be prepared for the answer. One never knows what's going to come out of a kid's mouth. Their simplistic ways seem to get the better of us adults. With just one innocent phrase, and in a most humble manner, they can make adults feel quite foolish.

My English Lit professor in college said that Charles Dickens mastered the art of marketing his own works. He went on to explain that Dickens knew any story about a child at the mercy of an evil adult, whereby the child outsmarted the adult thereby causing the adult to look like a fool, would sell. Turned out to be genius on his part. He knew what people loved to read.

Dickens' novels such as *Oliver Twist, Nicholas Nickleby, The Life and Adventures of Martin Chuzzlewit, David Copperfield*, as well as Mark Twain's *Huck Finn*, all depict kids at the mercy of adults, with the kids coming out the winners or heroes, if you will. The smash hit movie *Home Alone* is a perfect example of a kid outsmarting evil adults and making them look foolish. It didn't end there because *Home Alone 2* and *Home Alone 3* were also big hits. The list of kid-verses-adult movies goes on and on.

Why does this type of entertainment sell? My thought is adults, evil or good, are the ones in control. They call the shots, leaving kids with little to no say over what happens to them. However, when the adult is particularly evil, the reader or the audience cheers when the kid wins. We naturally pull for the underdog. It's entertainment at its best.

Art Linkletter knew where the entertainment lived in his television program, *House Party*, which began in the '40s and continued on until the '60s. The most well-known part of the show included the segment entitled "Kids Say the Darndest Things." It became so popular that the segment actually developed into a series by the same name.

Art Linkletter interviewed school children and then stood back and let their answers do the entertaining. The children ranged in age from five to ten. For those who remember the program, you'll remember its huge success. If you never saw the program, I would encourage you to find a DVD or video of the show. You'll be the better for it. But be prepared for your face and sides to hurt from laughing. Art went on to write a series of books and called them, of course, *Kids Say the Darndest Things*.

Art Linkletter understood that asking a child a question left the field wide open for almost any kind of response and typically made for hilarious television. Of course he possessed a talent for bringing out the kid in a kid. Most times he was more surprised at the answers than the audience.

With *Kids Say the Darndest Things* in mind, I thought it might be fun to interview my granddaughter, Skye, who, at the time of the interview was eight years old. She's quite the character, and probably one of the funniest kids I've ever known.

As I pondered over what sort of questions to ask her, I thought it might be fun to see how she would answer a series of questions based on politics, since I'm of the opinion that kids could run our country better than the adults running it now.

So why not? She's highly qualified. Her resume is quite extensive. She's very well read. Books are her life. She sees beyond herself and believes life is meant to be enjoyed, thus allowing very little time for looking back.

I approached her with the idea. "Skye, let's pretend you're running for President of the United States. Do you think you might like to do that someday?"

Her response. "Sure! Why not?"

Why not, indeed. I got the distinct feeling she actually

entertained the thought before I ever mentioned it. I found her "why not" response amusing, indicating her confidence in the fact that she could do the job. Completely unruffled by the concept posed to her, she sat with me ready to answer any question I hurled her way. Keep in mind, these responses are her own, in her own words, and presented as she actually said them. The interview went like this:

Interviewer: "Candidate Skye, I understand you decided to run for President of the United States. I would like to ask you some questions about your candidacy. My first question is: What are your plans to make the United States better?"

Candidate Skye: "I would build homes for people who need homes. I'm going to get home builders to build brick houses so that tornadoes won't hit their houses and break them. I would make the stores a little bit cheaper so that you could get some things on sale. Gas costs too much money, and sometimes people don't have enough money to pay for all the gas. The President should do something about that. I would tell the people who make the gas to stop charging so much money for the gas. They would have to do it because I would be the President. I would build more schools because some schools are running out of business."

Interviewer: "If you are elected President of the United States, how will you make life better for children?"

Candidate Skye: "I would make their clothes and toys cheaper for them. Probably because some of their toys are breaking, and they need new ones. I would make the children's beds only cost $20 or maybe not that much. I would set up a foundation for kids who need money. If a city doesn't have any games, the other cities that have games that they don't play with anymore, then they can give them to the President, and the President can give them to the cities who don't have any games for their children."

Interviewer: "What will you do as President of the United States to make schools safer and better?"

Candidate Skye: "If a school doesn't have a door, the people who built the school will have to come back and build the school a door. All the new schools that are being built have to be built with bricks. If a school is already built, they can just leave it like it is. The lunches at schools should not cost very much because they are getting too high. All the classrooms need to be separated because some schools have doors in between them that are broken, and sometimes the other class is too loud and it bothers the other class because they can't concentrate on what they're doing.

"I would like to have the teachers make it fun when they're teaching math. I think that the schools need more fun stuff on the playgrounds so that it's more fun to play. I would like the lunch room to have more carrots and more apples that don't have any bruises on them. The desks need to be bigger because they aren't big enough to put all your stuff in when the teacher tells you to make your desk neater. I think homework is good because it helps you to understand what the teacher has been talking about. I don't think you should have homework on Friday because kids need to rest their brain over the weekend, just in case they need to use their brains over the weekend to remind their parents about what they need to do."

Interviewer: "Do you have any thoughts on our current healthcare system?"

Candidate Skye: "I think that it cost too much money to go to see the doctor. If I was the President, I would make it not cost so much. If a person doesn't have enough money to go to see the doctor, then the doctor should let them come and see him anyway, and if they have just a little bit of money, the doctor should let them give them however much money they have. When you don't feel good, it makes you feel even badder if you don't have any money and can't go to the doctor. It should be easy to go to the doctor so that you can feel better. That would make everybody happy."

Interviewer: "How many days in a week do you think people should work?"

Candidate Skye: "People should work five days a week. But only Monday through Friday and they should not work on the weekends. People who like to work on the weekends should work, and people who don't like to work on the weekends shouldn't have to work. Hospital people should work on the weekends. The store people should work on the weekends. Firemen should work on the weekends. And the police should work on the weekends. So if you're one of those people, you should know that you'll have to work on the weekends. If you don't want to work on the weekends, then you shouldn't be one of those people and just find a job so that you can just work during the week and not on the weekends."

Interviewer: "On your very first day as President of the United States what do you think you will do?"

Candidate Skye: "The first thing I'm going to do is sign papers I need to sign. I would sign papers like contracts. I'll probably make a speech that will last forty-eight minutes. I'll talk about helping people, taking care of the country, and working hard. I won't redecorate the office. I'll just leave it like it is 'cause it would cost too much money."

Interviewer: "Do you plan to take a vacation during your time as President? If so, how many days will you take off?"

Candidate Skye: "I'll take a little vacation. It'll last about nine days. I won't take a vacation every year, and I'll only take nine days the whole time I'm President. I'll take my vacation at Six Flags."

Interviewer: "How much money do you think the President of the United States should make?"

Candidate Skye: "I think the President should make $8,000 a year because that's all the President needs to make since they get to live in the White House and don't have to pay anything to live there."

Interviewer: "What do you intend to do for poor people and elderly people?"

Candidate Skye: "I'll build houses for the poor people. I'm going to make sure they have food. Everybody in the White House will give food to the poor. We'll buy them a fridge and then buy the food. If there's a playground somewhere that nobody's using, I'll give that playground to the poor people who have kids. The people in the White House will give the poor people beds to go in their houses. When I'm the President, I'll ask businesses to give jobs to the poor people so they can work and make their own money, 'cause it makes you feel good when you make your own money, 'cause you can buy your own stuff and then people won't have to give you anything. I'll help the elderly people cross the street. I'll help them check their mail. If they don't know how to turn on their TV, I'll help them. I'll help them go to the doctor when they're sick, and if they're really sick, I'll help them go to the hospital. I think I would like to drive to get them myself. I'll go shopping with them if they need somebody to go with them. When you're the President you can do stuff like that, and it'll make people happy to see you."

Interviewer: "How many years do you think a person should be allowed to be the President?"

Candidate Skye: "I think they should only be President for six years. But if they don't do good, they should have to go home and not be the President anymore."

Interviewer: "Who do you think the best President has been so far?"

Candidate Skye: "The Presidents I like best are George Washington, Abraham Lincoln, John F. Kennedy, and George Bush. I like George Bush because he made really good speeches, and he looks like a nice man, and he has a farm that looks pretty fun to go and visit. I like John F. Kennedy. John F. Kennedy was shot in Dallas, Texas. He was riding in a car. I like Abraham Lincoln a lot because he freed the slaves. He was shot, too. He was shot when he was at the theatre watching a play. I like George Washington because he was the first President, and it was sad that he died of a very bad cold."

Interviewer: "What does it mean when a country has to go to war?"

Candidate Skye: "It means that soldiers have to fight for their country so that people can keep their homes, and they have to fight for America's freedom. I think it's sad when you have to go to war."

Interviewer: "What do you think would be the best part about being President?"

Candidate Skye: "The best part would be to live in the White House. Another best part would be that you could say speeches, and people have to listen to you and you can help people."

Interviewer: "Do you think it is okay for the President of the United States to visit other countries? If so, why? If not, why not?"

Candidate Skye: "Yes, because you can help people in other countries. You can also give speeches. I would have meetings with the other presidents, and we could talk and go swimming. I would give them some gifts."

Interviewer: "If the President could live anywhere else other than at the White House, where do you think the President could live?"

Candidate Skye: "The President could live at a hotel. If you had a best friend, you could spend the night with your best friend. You could even spend the night with your parents or grandparents. The President could just live in a regular house."

Interviewer: "Do you think that anyone can become President?"

Candidate Skye: "Yes, but they have to be a grown-up."

Interviewer: "How old do you think the President of the United States should be? Why do you believe that?"

Candidate Skye: "I think you would have to be thirty-eight years old or higher 'cause you're done with school."

Interviewer: "Do you think it is important that the President know a whole lot about the history of our country? If so, why? If not, why not?"

Candidate Skye: "Yes, 'cause it'll help with the future. That way we'll know about wars and how houses looked like and about other Presidents so we won't do what they did and be copying them."

Interviewer: "How many years of school do you think a person should have to attend in order to be the President of the United States? Why do you believe that?"

Candidate Skye: "I think they should have to go to school for twenty years, 'cause you need to be smart to be the President."

Interviewer: "My last question is this. Why do you want to be the President of the United States?"

Candidate Skye: "I want to be President, 'cause I want to help people and I want to give speeches and I want to build houses for people and I want to help little kids, 'cause sometimes they need the President to help them. I would also want to have a little fun in the White House, too, 'cause it's so big, and it would take a long time to look at all the rooms. It would be fun to run around all over the White House. I think I would like to ride my bike all around the White House so I could look around better. But the first reason I want to be President is so that I can help the people take care of each other and take care of themselves. I think they need somebody to do that, 'cause sometimes it makes you feel better when somebody helps you. That way you can learn how to do stuff."

I came away from the interview a much more enlightened person, convinced Skye would make a great President even at the ripe old age of eight. No prejudice leanings whatsoever.

Whether you gleaned from this interview that Skye is a conservative or a liberal, it really doesn't matter. What matters is that she possesses great insight into giving of herself—a lesson most politicians would do well to learn.

As Skye and I chatted, I realized her main concern continued to be the cost of things. Her goal centered on helping those who could not help themselves. She also believed in helping people *do* for themselves, thereby giving them a sense of accomplishment. I agreed with her on all counts. Things *do* cost too much, and we *do* need to help each other more bearing in mind that it's best to help in a way that allows people to help themselves. This concept begins with the President and filters down.

I decided to do a bit of research to ascertain what other kids thought about our country and the role the President plays. I thought it would be interesting to see if they shared any of Skye's views.

Letter-writing is the best way for people to express themselves. Likewise, reading letters written by others is the best way to discover how people really feel. I found the Internet jammed packed with letters from kids to various Presidents over the years.

I discovered letters written to Abraham Lincoln, George Washington, Herbert Hoover, Franklin D. Roosevelt, Harry S. Truman, Lyndon B. Johnson, Richard M. Nixon, John F. Kennedy, and George W. Bush. They proved to be very interesting reading.

I took note of the fact that a common thread ran through all of them—they didn't seem above asking for help from the President and sharing with the President their inner most feelings. Amazingly, the letters' down-to-earth manner brought the sitting President into their world. Like my granddaughter, they were all concerned with the cost of things, even back to George Washington. Things like

The Great Depression, war, job loss, a woman President, concern for the health of the President, and the economy were all matters of concern to kids because they were living through it and saw its effects.

These kids shared their thoughts and feelings with men who were at the top of the ladder when it comes to power. Even though each man held the title of President of the most powerful country in the world, these children spoke to them in their writings as if they were speaking to an old friend. And they always spoke to things that would help their family, rarely, if ever, asking for anything for themselves. How could one not be touched by that?

Kids have a way of cutting to the heart of issues. They're not easily impressed with things like status or how far up the food chain a person might be. Even the President of the United States appears to be just the guy who lives in that great big white house, when seen through the eyes of a child.

Kids Say the Darndest Things showed America that kids have their own opinions, and think nothing of sharing them with whoever has the guts to ask the question. I saw this to be true in my childhood, as well.

When I was five, I appeared on the *Howdy Doody Show*. My mother beamed with pride. She dressed me up in a ridiculous white frilly dress, black patent shoes and lacy white socks—all of which I hated. She attached a bow bigger than my head to my *pixie* haircut. I wanted to spit!

We arrived at the television station along with ten other kids just as dressed up and miserable as I. Mothers and fathers scurried about as if we were each making our debut on our own television program.

The show's staff ushered the children onto the set as the parents sat safely tucked away on the other side of the studio so as not to interfere with the production. As the lights went up, and the *Howdy Doody Show* began, all the mothers and fathers sat on the edge of their seats, holding their breath, terrified at the prospect of what might come out of their kid's mouth once the questions started to fly.

Then suddenly *my* turn arrived. When asked what my father did for a living, I proudly stood up and stated loudly, "HE DRINKS LIQUOR!" My mother fell out of her chair.

Actually, my father, an Army Sergeant at the time, worked weekends at the NCO Club as a bartender to make extra money. In kid language that meant *he drinks liquor.* If memory serves me, the entire cast and crew laughed so hard they quickly cut to a commercial. That ended my thirty seconds of fame. I don't remember ever being allowed to return to television after that.

When we think of the things kids hear or see, then interpret, it should give us pause.

I knew before I ever sat down with Skye that she would be the one teaching me a thing or two. I found it strange how her concerns and goals were pretty much the same as those who came before her, from 1789—the beginning of George Washington's Presidency—right up to today.

A guy by the name of Robert Fulghum wrote a book entitled *All I Really Need to Know I Learned in Kindergarten.* It's very much worth the read. When my oldest daughter attended elementary school, one of the parents stood up at a PTA meeting and read aloud the things Fulghum said he learned in kindergarten and how it helped shape his life. If we, as adults, adhered to each of the lessons mentioned in the book, there would be no need for us to take any medications for blood pressure. Therefore, keeping our life in balance is the best way to accomplish that.

The Bible speaks to us not only about the responsibilities of children, but also how we learn from them. In Psalm 127:3–5 we read: "Children are a heritage from the Lord, offspring a reward from him. Like arrows in the hands of a warrior are children born in one's youth. Blessed is the man whose quiver is full of them. They will not be put to shame when they contend with their opponents in court."

The Bible also speaks to us about how we treat children. This verse is particularly close to my heart as I know its power first hand. Proverbs 22:6: "Start children off on the way they should go, and even when they are old they will not turn from it."

In Matthew 19:14 Jesus shows His love for children: "Jesus said, 'Let the little children come to me, and do not hinder them, for the kingdom of heaven belongs to such as these.'"

Proverbs 20:11 also reminds us: "Even small children are known by their actions, so is their conduct really pure and upright?"

It only follows that we take great care of those little ones the Lord entrusts to our charge. They harbor great knowledge inside their tiny bodies, and they welcome the opportunity to share it with anyone willing to take the time to sit and listen.

As I read and reread Skye's responses, it occurred to me that she knew exactly the role of the President—to care for and to serve the people. And if you get a chance to throw in a few speeches from time to time, then that's okay, too.

Amazing how when I think I've got it all figured out these eye opening moments hit me and God brings me back to His Word. In that Word I find what we're all meant to see.

It appears in 1Timothy 3:1–5: "Here is a trustworthy saying: Whoever aspires to be an overseer desires a noble task. Now the overseer is to be above reproach, faithful to his wife, temperate, self-controlled, respectable, hospitable, able to teach, not given to drunkenness, not violent but gentle, not quarrelsome, not a lover of money. He must manage his own family well and see that his children obey him, and he must do so in a manner worthy of full respect. (If anyone does not know how to manage his own family, how can he take care of God's church?)" Funny, Skye knew this all along.

So, here's the message from Skye, the Word, Mr. Linkletter, *The Howdy Doody Show,* Mr. Dickens, Mr. Twain, and Mr. Fulghum: Kids always win when up against evil adults. Don't ask if you don't want to hear the truth. A kid's point of view is all that matters to the kid. Manage your life well. Remember what you learned in kindergarten. Help those who can't help themselves. Teach people to fish so they can provide for themselves. Hold a person responsible for their actions. Finally, share your thoughts and questions with the President—he'll appreciate it.

I must admit I loved every second Skye and I spent together talking politics. That's why it's easy to see the reason I say—Skye for President!

CHAPTER TWELVE

The Reason Doing It My Way Doesn't Work

ONE DAY WHILE OUT running errands I had the radio on, as I usually do. I enjoy singing along with the songs I love best—windows down as the wind blows through my hair, although it embarrasses my children. This particular day—one of God's beautiful ones—found me rocking to the beat of the tambourine, all settled into my happy place. "My Way" by Frank Sinatra came on. Hot flash! Yes, this is the type of station I listen to, not the hard rock/hip-hopper type—tempting as they are. I go to a time and place when they sang actual words, and the words they sang were understood.

Like the song says, doing it my way seemed to be my theme for quite some time. Over the years I learned that doing things my way only got me into trouble. At the time I insisted on going this route, I didn't care about the consequences. I wanted to do it my way, and that's all that mattered.

Growing up an only child, I developed an edge that allowed me to do things my way and stay out of trouble at the same time. Well, sometimes. But then my daddy happened to be an only child, too, so he had my number. I thought myself a master of the art. The reality turned out to be my daddy giving me just enough rope to hang myself. And hang myself I did, many times. There are rope burns left behind to prove it.

While traveling down a road of my own making, it never mattered who got in the way. It only meant they were doing it wrong and it usually just made me angry. Only idiots weren't doing things my way. The truth is, they were doing it their way, too. See, people who bask in the glow of doing it their own way typically don't care about how others go about doing things.

For example, I remember this kid who lived next door to us when I was five years old. The only reason I remember him so vividly is because I hated his guts. In fact, everyone in the neighborhood hated this kid. I'm convinced even his parents hated him because his mom put him outside in the yard for hours every day of his life. His mother explained to my mother if she didn't leave him outside she'd kill him. Yeah, well, it was the 50s.

I remember him as vulgar, destructive, and bratty. He called me Rõgina. I knew my name wasn't Rõgina. Five-year-olds know their name. Any time I would go outside and see him, I would run back into the house.

This kid never wanted to stop to go to the bathroom while playing outside. So he would wrap his legs around a tree and hold it until the urge passed or he wet his pants. I never could understand that about him. When his mom saw him wrapped around a tree, she would come outside, grab him by the scruff of the neck and take him inside. Parents were allowed to do things like that to their kids back then.

I can't remember his name, but I remember his face. I've often wondered what happened to that kid. He's probably doing time in a federal prison somewhere. Some might say he just wanted to do things his way. I agree. But his way got him a whipping. Another one of those 50s things.

Francis Albert Sinatra was well known for being an incredible singer. His voice, his style and his attitude set him apart. His voice made young girls swoon. His style made young men jealous. His attitude made him famous. It didn't take long before people were calling him Ol' Blue Eyes or the Chairman of the Board. I refer to him as the original *Bom*, whatever that means. I never really knew very much about him other than I loved his voice. Nothing else really interested me.

Getting back to my beautiful day, Frank came on and "My Way" filled the airwaves. It's a beautiful song. Even though I've heard it a thousand times, I never tire of it. I know every word. Singing along with Frank and swaying back and forth. What more could there be?

Mr. Sinatra didn't do too badly for himself because he received eleven Grammy Awards, starred in some movies, won one Oscar, and received a nomination for another. Most considered him a true performer, doing it his way throughout his entire life. He died in 1998. I've always admired the man's talent. And what a talent.

If you read the lyrics to "My Way," you'll discover it's a powerful song and well worth the listen. But seeing the words written down, I find them different from the way I hear them. The word *stubbornness* comes to mind when pondering this song. Let's not go off the deep end thinking I'm anti-*my way*. Nothing could be further from the truth. I'm the original *my way* kid. But the song speaks for itself. Check out the words. They might be worth the time.

In the Book of Jeremiah 7:23–24 we find this: "but I gave them this command: Obey me, and I will be your God and you will be my people. Walk in obedience to all I command you, that it may go well with you. But they did not listen or pay attention; instead, they followed the stubborn inclinations of their evil hearts. They went backward and not forward." Kinda nips doing it my way in the bud.

I did it my way a lot during my growing up years. In fact, I continued doing it my way into my early adulthood. That is, until I had children. Then it became *their way*. That only lasted until I learned how to be an effective parent, and then I still did it their way. Not really, but I let them think they were doing it their way. Now that they're grown, I no longer need to do it their way. Now that *I've* grown, I've learned how to do it *God's way*. It's funny to look back over our lives and take note of the times we did it our way.

Here's my list of the top 12, in no particular order:

1. I closed a bumble bee up in a flower using my thumb and forefinger.
   RESULT: I got stung.
2. My cousin and I got into the fireworks stash and decided to light a couple of them.
   RESULT: A firecracker went off in my hand.
3. I took a bottle of soda out of the fridge and shook it up before I opened it.
   RESULT: It spewed all over me.
4. When I used to smoke, I lit a cigarette with the car lighter while driving with the windows down.
   RESULT: A live ash flew off and almost set me on fire.
5. I decided to put my makeup on (specifically mascara) while driving and had to slam on brakes.
   RESULT: I almost poked my eye out.
6. I ran off and got married at the age of eighteen without my parents' knowledge or consent.
   RESULT: The marriage ended in divorce.
7. I dropped out of college because I thought I didn't need it.
   RESULT: I have had to work harder and longer to prove myself.
8. I cut across a field that my parents told me to stay away from while walking to school.
   RESULT: A bull with very sharp horns chased me and missed the seat of my pants by a fraction of an inch.
9. I stole a piece of chocolate candy out of the local drug store.
   RESULT: I threw up for an hour after I ate it.
10. Even though the bathroom sink stood taller than me, I attempted to wash my feet and legs in it.
    RESULT: I fell, busted my chin on the sink, had to be taken to the hospital, and received seven stitches.

11. I went running through the backyard not paying attention to my surroundings.
    RESULT: *I practically hung myself on the clothesline.*
12. At the age of seven, I told my mother to shut-up.
    RESULT: *I don't remember what happened after that.*

As you can see, doing it my way didn't work out so well. Even now, when I relapse and try to do things my way, consequences still happen. There's an overabundance of people out there doing it their way, too, and from what I've seen, it doesn't work for them either. Like the bad guys on the once televised program *America's Dumbest Criminals*. They discover pretty quickly that doing it their way doesn't work for them at all. Jail is their result.

I'm certain God looks at me on a regular basis and thinks, "Did I actually create that one?" Doing it my way usually left me with some embarrassing moments, but it never stopped me from doing it my way again anyway. Shame on me.

What do we reflect on when we think of the times in our lives when we've gone our way in spite of others' counsel? How did those situations turn out? In Proverbs 13:13 we read: "Whoever scorns instruction will pay for it, but whoever respects a command is rewarded." That's the key to why most of us like doing it our way. We ain't too keen on the instruction part. It's also the reason doing it my way doesn't work.

When I found myself despising the instruction, I certainly paid the penalty. Over the years, I've learned to obey the commandment. Learning the hard way is an American pastime I fear. All one need do to verify that statement is to turn on the television.

Wouldn't it be nice if we would obey the commandment first? But then we wouldn't know the pleasures of *doing it my way*. If we all made a list of the times we despised the instruction and paid the penalty, I'm sure the majority of us, including myself, could come up with more than twelve. Some of us are still adding to that list.

For those who allow God to walk with them through their decision making, theirs is a much easier path. For those of us who tend to ignore God's offer of assistance, well, our paths tend to get rockier. In our defense, those rockier times make us realize the reason doing it my way doesn't work.

CHAPTER THIRTEEN

Ella

FAMILY SECRETS CAN PACK a wallop. They're like old baggage you carry around throughout your life. You can't seem to put it down. It tarnishes everything it touches. My grandmother, Ella, left behind a dark secret that cast a shadow over my entire family.

Ella Morgan Stone died at age forty-five. She was my grandmother. Documents indicate the year of her birth as 1886 and the year of her death as 1931. Twenty-one years passed from the year of her death to the year of my birth. It would stand to reason I never had the pleasure of meeting her, although I very much wish I could say I knew her in the same way I knew my maternal grandmother.

My parents named me Ellan Regina. My father wanted a part of my name to reflect his mother's. That's the only part of my grandmother I knew about at the beginning.

I could be politically correct and say my grandmother's life on this earth came to an untimely end. But I've never been one to stoop to political correctness. Neither fate nor God nor the act of any other person ended my grandmother's life. Not even an illness. My grandmother, for whatever reason, decided her life held no value. And in the year 1931, when her son, my father, was only twelve years old, she took her own life.

I've been told by family members who knew Ella that she stood tall in stature like my father. She had dark hair and an olive complexion like my father. I've known about the dark hair and olive complexion my entire life. You see, my father owned a portrait of Ella. It hung on the wall in my parent's bedroom for as long as I can remember. It now hangs in my living room next to a portrait of William Callaway Stone, her husband and my grandfather.

William possessed the opposite appearance of Ella, with his strawberry blonde hair and a fair complexion; both of which showed off his Irish roots. He played the role of disciplinarian when it came to raising his son, my father. I met him only once, at the age of six weeks. I don't remember the meeting.

William, born April 26, 1888, died of a heart attack on April 20, 1953, just six days shy of his sixty-fifth birthday. Strangely enough, I possess a copy of his death and birth certificates. I found them in a box of papers after my father died. I found no papers in that box regarding my grandmother.

From what my father told me about his mother, baking, needlework, tatting (making lace), and gardening were her favorite pastimes. He remembered all the flowers in the yard as well as the ones in pots and flower boxes on their big front porch. He recalled she loved working with her hands and staying busy. They were very close.

She pampered him and protected him, he being her only child. I'm sure it became a bit stifling for him at times.

In every childhood picture of my father, I find him dressed in white or in a sailor suit with carefully starched collar. She liked to dress him this way. Not an ounce of dirt to be found anywhere. Perfectionism runs thick in this family.

The details leading up to Ella's suicide have, over the years, become a bit blurry and distorted in places. My father, however, remembered the day of her death with perfect clarity.

He was in school when a family member, not his father, came to take him home. When told of his mother's death, devastation set in. Years later, upon learning the cause of her death, anger took over. I believe in some way he knew all along.

I don't know all the details. Like I said, the story became blurry. Some said they never saw it coming. Others said she seemed moody and despondent. As to the method, that too remained disputed among family members. Some said she hanged herself. Others said she used gas from the kitchen stove. Her death certificate, eventually discovered, read, "Gunshot wound to the head."

For me, the method seems unimportant. It's the why I want to understand. She obviously adored her child. No one told stories of a rocky marriage. The only thing I'm certain of is the scar her actions left on my father. To add insult to injury, Ella took her life during the Christmas season. Some legacy. Sometimes my own anger creeps in.

Throughout my growing up years, I often wondered why my father always seemed on edge, angry even, over Christmas.

Around my middle twenties, I learned the reason quite by accident.

I had scheduled a complete physical. The doctor's office required a detailed questionnaire regarding my medical history. One of the questions on the questionnaire read: "Has anyone in your immediate family committed suicide? If so, who?"

I happened to be sitting at my parents' dining room table while completing the questionnaire and happened to read the question out loud. Shock ran through me as my father abruptly answered, "Yes."

The tone in his voice held great anger shaded with deep sorrow. I innocently asked, "Who?" In the same angered and sorrowful voice, my father announced quite loudly, "My Mother," and left the room. I almost fell out of my chair at this revelation. Based on my father's reaction, I knew better than to follow behind, asking questions.

A couple days later I dared to broach the subject with my mother. The obvious first question: why keep something like this from me? My mother said neither of them ever wanted me to know. Strange. We're talking about my grandmother, right? Pretty important information to keep hidden from your only child. The revelation explained so much. Like my father's holiday mood swings.

We never talked about it again.

I know suicide is intentional. It's when a person takes his or her own life. No antonyms exist for the word "suicide." Did this apply to my grandmother? Intentional self-destruction?

What goes through a person's mind when contemplating suicide? As it pertains to my grandmother, my question still remains.

Why?

Later in my father's life, when he and I had gained more years, he almost spoke to me of his mother's death, but stopped. He told my husband in years past, how family rumors claimed his mother committed suicide, but he remained unconvinced and believed other family members might think the same. He even went so far as to insinuate to my husband and to my mother (earlier in their marriage) that he believed his father murdered her. Yet, his response to my doctor questionnaire contradicted these feelings he shared. His previous outburst of admission to me of his mother's suicide left me with the belief that my father knew his mother took her own life, yet he found himself desperate to think otherwise. And in an effort to rid himself of his anger toward his mother, he needed to make a case that the suicide never happened. But happen it did. My grandmother left behind a child who would carry the pain of her actions to his own grave.

I find myself hard-pressed to locate the actual word "suicide" in the Bible. I do know the Bible speaks about six people who committed suicide—Saul, Abimelech (Saul's armor-bearer), Ahithophel, Zimri, and Judas. Some believe Samson committed suicide. He *did* tear down the walls of the Temple knowing he would lose his own life as well. Most believe he intended to sacrifice himself to kill the Philistines. We read Samson's story in Judges 16.

First Samuel 31:4 records Saul's suicide. In Judges 9:52–54,

Abimelek is referred to as an assisted suicide. We learn of Saul's armor-bearer in 1 Samuel 31:5 and find the suicide of Ahithophel in 2 Samuel 17:23. Next we learn about Zimri dying by his own hand in 1 Kings 16:18. And who could forget Judas, the betrayer of Jesus. I secretly disdain Judas. He seems such a weasel, easily swayed by the smell of money. If totally honest, I admit thinking suicide too good for Judas. Matthew 27:3–5 tells the story.

For Judas, it appears suicide became an easy way out of a dire situation. A situation he got himself into, fueled by his greed. I see him as a coward, who, at the last minute, became remorseful and turned to suicide to ease the consequences he feared and couldn't face. My tolerance level for Judas dips far below the normal level for people of his caliber. But that's just me. Most likely a sentiment of mine that needs much work.

From what I've learned throughout my years in Bible study, church, and Sunday school, suicide equals murder—self-murder. These teachings proclaimed the only one qualified to decide how and when an individual should die is God and God alone. The choice is not meant to be ours.

Mounds and mounds of papers exist recounting why people commit suicide. Questions emerge as to whether a Christian who commits suicide will go to hell. Does God forgive His child who experiences a moment of weakness and commits suicide? There's a vault full of questions. I find the answer in 1 Corinthians 6:19–20. "Do you not know that your bodies are temples of the Holy Spirit, who is in you, whom you have received from God? You are not your own; you were bought at a price. Therefore honor God with your bodies." These verses tell me suicide is wrong. Unforgiveable? Only God can answer that. I suspect although we give up on ourselves, He never gives up on us.

Upon discovering my grandmother's suicide, I must admit

anger took over. Although I never even knew her, my anger toward her grew for what I considered playing God with her life. A life she owed to God. A life that belonged to God. My heart ached on behalf of my father and how her act affected his entire life.

I suspect, however, people who commit suicide feel helpless to fix their sorrow. I'm sure mental illness plays a heavy hand in suicide, pushing people to make a decision that burns like wildfire through a family causing pain to all those left behind.

As I look into the deep, dark eyes that stare back at me from Ella's portrait, I make up stories about her life, always stopping short of the day of her death. I picture her in her garden or sitting by the fire doing needlework or baking bread in the family kitchen. I imagine getting to know her and listening to her tell silly stories about my father's childhood. I find myself studying every line of her face and taking note of her beauty.

Before I know it, several minutes pass as I stand gazing at the woman in the portrait. A woman I never knew. As I wipe the tears away, I find myself asking out loud, "Why? Why did you do it, Ella? What were you thinking? How could you hurt your son like that?" Then, sadly, the anger returns.

It's so very strange, that fine line between love and hate or anger and sorrow. I'm quite sure my father walked that line throughout his life. A part of him literally hated my grandmother for leaving him that way. And the part that loved her beyond words struggled with the hate and the whys causing him to vacillate between belief and uncertainty. Without doubt, my father felt great remorse for the times he hated my grandmother. The guilt over those feelings ate him alive.

The complexities of suicide are numerous. The guilt the family suffers wondering how they might have contributed to their loved one's choice. The shame of facing friends who know about the suicide. The isolation one feels for fear of being spiritually alienated. The self loathing one might feel because they couldn't stop the act.

As the years have passed since I discovered this family secret, I can finally admit that even though I never knew her, a big part of me loves her dearly and mourns the day she chose death over life. Still, under the surface, the rage remains. I don't like how it makes me feel and often wish I felt differently. God knows my heart, and I reach out for Him during these times of anger.

I still wonder. I wonder if Ella thought of her child as she prepared to end her life. I wonder if she thought of anything other than ending whatever pain or despair she happened to be in at the moment. I also wonder why someone could not have helped Ella find the hope and joy in living.

I overflow with questions I may never find answers to. Answers I'm not certain I even want to hear. So where does that leave me? Angry at my grandmother for the rest of my life? This woman I never knew? I certainly hope not. I watched what anger did to my father. I watched him turn into a moody, short-tempered man every year during the entire month of December. Wishing now I might have made those times easier for him had I only known.

I have to draw back to God. He knows what my grandmother carried around in her heart, for I surely don't. He alone knows the deep pain that drove her to suicide. Although suicide is a terrible tragedy, an act that causes heartbreak and anger, I'm certain it doesn't negate the Lord's love or His act of redemption. On the cross, Jesus paid our price. God's grace applies to all who put their trust in Him.

The actions of one woman rippled out like the circles in a pond after a rock hits the surface. Ella's ripples wash over the lives of those who never even knew her. I think of faith and wonder if it played any sort of role in her life. I know how it sustains me.

When troubles come my way, and I've faced more than I care to recount, I cling to verses that give me comfort. In particular, I remember Psalm 34:17–20: "The righteous cry out, and the Lord hears them; he delivers them from all their troubles. The Lord is close to the brokenhearted and saves those who are crushed in spirit. The righteous person may have many troubles, but the Lord delivers him from them all; he protects all his bones, not one of them will be broken."

If I could reach back in time and somehow stop my grandmother's actions, I wouldn't hesitate. If I could take away the agony that plagued her, I wouldn't hesitate. If I could take away a lifetime of pain from my father, I wouldn't hesitate. I guess it comes to this: my life would be sweeter if I'd only known you . . . Ella.

1 Corinthians 6:19-20
Psalm 34:17-20

CHAPTER FOURTEEN

When Mr. Matthews Went to Washington
In Honor of Technical Staff Sergeant
Byron Waitcel Matthews

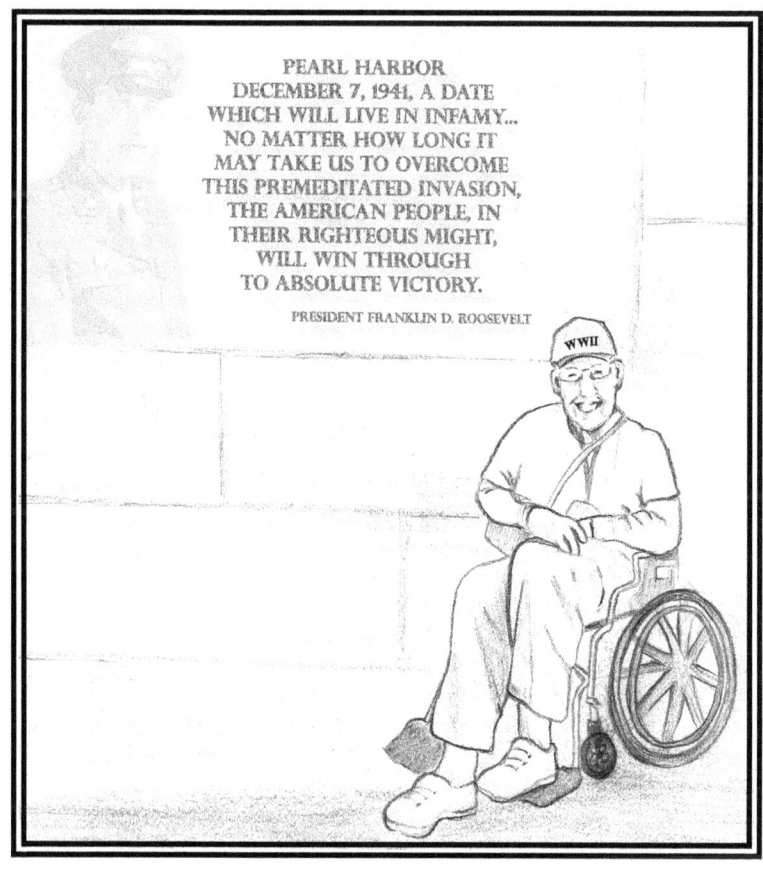

BYRON WAITCEL MATTHEWS FOUND himself drafted into the Army in January of 1944. At the age of twenty-three, he considered himself just an ordinary guy with his own extraordinary goals planned out. That didn't include a hitch in the Army.

We all make plans that get interrupted. It's called life. I've always believed that God laughs loudest when we tell him our plans. We seem to think our future is entirely up to us as we map out each step.

Until his draft notice arrived, young Mr. Matthews found himself gainfully employed. In January of 1942, he started working for the Civil Aeronautics Administration or the CAA, which is now the Federal Aviation Administration or the FAA, as an aircraft communicator. He had turned twenty-one. World War II, already in progress, actually began on September 1, 1939. The United States didn't get involved until Japan attacked Pearl Harbor on December 7, 1941.

When President Roosevelt called for a response to the Pearl Harbor attack, young Byron got lucky. He received an occupational deferment. But his luck didn't hold out. In January of 1944, he found himself drafted right along with every other guy who happened to be breathing at the time. No longer an ordinary guy, young Matthews now called himself a soldier. I call him a hero.

I don't refer to him as a hero because he received a truckload of medals. I refer to him as a hero because he loved his country enough to fight for it when asked.

Technical Staff Sergeant Matthews joined the guys of the *3186 Signal Service Battalion Company A* and promptly started his tour of England, France, Germany, Belgium, Luxemburg, and Japan. Thirteen Command Posts existed throughout Europe. This group of guys serviced eleven of them. They operated a communications system that included the most up-to-date equipment of the time. On September 2, 1945, World War II ended. Matthews proudly served his country from 1944–1946.

Technical Staff Sergeant Byron Waitcel Matthews earned a few medals: the Good Conduct Medal, the Asiatic-Pacific Campaign Medal, the European-African-Middle Eastern Campaign Medal with two bronze service stars, the WWII Victory Medal, the Army of Occupation Medal with Germany clasp and Japan clasp, the Philippine Liberation Ribbon, the Honorable Service Lapel Button WWII, and the Sharpshooter Badge with Rifle Bar. Not too shabby.

During the years that followed the war, he never saw his name in the newspapers, never appeared on the nightly news circuits or the ever-popular late-night talk shows. Never even appeared before the President or shook his hand. But he wore his medals with pride. Medals now safely tucked away inside a shadow box that hangs on the wall. He is a hero.

What happens to heroes when the years roll by and there's little to no recognition for their sacrifices? One might think they become bitter, turn away from their country, or wish they never served in the first place. What good did it do, anyway? Yet anyone who knows anything about heroes knows they aren't made that way. The unsung heroes are like any other hero—noble. In our culture, too often the term nobility is reserved for the famous. Its graces are saved for those seen on television, in the movies, on stage, in the sports arenas, and yes, in government. This is an insult to nobleness.

Technical Staff Sergeant Byron Waitcel Matthews served his country with pride, standing shoulder-to-shoulder with every other soldier who went before him and who will come after him. It's an elite club of men and women who watch over us every day, protect us, fight for us, and secure the freedoms we enjoy and take for granted way too many times.

On October 8, 2008, now private-citizen Mr. Matthews (age 87) went to Washington in honor of the young Technical Staff Sergeant Byron Waitcel Matthews. Seventy others from his surrounding area of Georgia accompanied him in honor of their own accomplishments. They were the Honor Flight of Fayette County, Inc., Georgia.

They arrived at the Methodist Church in Fayette County Georgia at 6:00 a.m. (that would be the *early* part of the day). At 7:00 a.m. they rode buses to the Atlanta Hartsfield International Airport to board a plane scheduled to leave at 9:40 a.m. to take them on a one-day adventure. One that proved to be a step back in history—a trip down memory lane to a time and place where heroes were made.

Aboard the plane that flew the seventy veterans from Georgia were one doctor, four nurses, and a handful of EMT's. Weeks prior to the flight, the veterans completed a medical history on themselves, taking into account their medications and their mobility capabilities—a ton of paperwork for a day of memories. I'm sure they all felt it to be a small price to pay.

They landed at the Reagan National Airport at 11:30 a.m. As they exited the plane, some walked on their own, some used canes or walkers, some sat in wheelchairs. A group of Servicemen who happened to be in the airport at the time stood in a line and shook the hand of every veteran who walked by. Pretty classy, I'd say.

The Honor Flight arranged the veterans into groups of two to three and then assigned each group a guardian. Technical Staff Sergeant Byron Waitcel Matthews called the guardian assigned to him his *Guardian Angel*. Ironic, I think, because once upon a time these very men were Guardian Angels to us all.

After making their way through the airport in Washington,

DC, they boarded buses that carried them to the National World War II Memorial, the memorial that took seventeen years to become a reality. It opened to the public on April 29, 2004.

When they arrived, they walked the grounds with approximately five hundred other veterans who were also visiting. Three tents were set up where the veterans were served box lunches. They stayed at the Memorial until 3:30 p.m. Then the seventy who arrived together got back on the buses and took a tour of Washington, DC. They arrived back at the Regan National Airport at 5:30 p.m.

A section of the airport, set up for dinner, was a welcomed sight. Afterwards, they boarded the plane and departed at 7:30 p.m., leaving behind a day filled with the joys of reminiscing. They arrived back at the Atlanta Hartsfield International Airport at around 10:00 p.m. At 11:00 p.m., they were back at the Methodist Church in Fayette County, Georgia. By the time Technical Staff Sergeant Byron Waitcel Matthews, now private-citizen Matthews, got home, the clock chimed 2:00 a.m.—the end to a long but fulfilling day.

When I think of all the military men and women I've known, I think of the sacrifices they and their families make in an effort for them to serve. It's an amazing feat of selflessness. We all walk on this ground due to the sacrifice of others, much like we go to be with our Father in Heaven because of the sacrifice of One.

Technical Staff Sergeant Byron Waitcel Matthews, along with my daddy, my daughter, my son-in-law, and others like them, risked their lives to defend and protect the United States of America. We owe it to them to take pride in this country, to fight for it, to protect it, to maintain its greatness, and to love it as they have.

As Galatians 6:2 reads: "Carry each other's burdens, and in this way you will fulfill the law of Christ." Our servicemen and women most definitely bear our burdens—twenty-four hours a day—seven days a week—three hundred and sixty-five days a year.

Psalm 144:1–2 tells us: "Praise be to the Lord my Rock, who trains my hands for war, my fingers for battle. He is my loving God and my fortress, my stronghold and my deliverer, my shield, in whom I take refuge, who subdues peoples under me." My father-in-law took these passages to heart as he served his country and carried them with him throughout his life.

On November 6, 2008, the planners held a reunion for the seventy who boarded the Honor Flight to Washington, DC. They came together again for a time of celebration and reminiscing. As a token of appreciation, they were given a DVD of their trip. A lump swelled up in my throat as I watched the faces of the men and women on the Honor Flight to Washington, DC in the video. I saw pride in their eyes, their smiles, and their walk. It oozed out of every orifice of their being. I found myself proud of all of them, even though I knew only one.

I watched intently, searching for now private-citizen Byron Waitcel Matthews, my father-in-law, to catch a glimpse of him. Suddenly he appeared, his *Guardian Angel* pushing him in his wheelchair; his head held high, grinning from ear to ear. Proud to be a part of this group of heroes and proud to be a part of the Honor Flight of Fayette County, Inc., Georgia. Most of all, proud to be an American Veteran. What a glorious day!

He remembered with clarity the four thousand gold stars on the Freedom Wall, each star representing one hundred soldiers who lost their lives in the service of their country during World War II. That's a total of four hundred thousand fallen heroes. These are heroes we owe a debt of gratitude we will never be able to repay. All we will ever be able to do is offer a heartfelt thank you, which seems quite lame.

The U.S. National World War II Memorial, the Korean War Veterans Memorial, and the Vietnam Veterans Memorial are all dedicated to those who served, and rightly so. As an American who always supported our military, I say it's a good and decent thing to give a little something back. To offer up these memorials in their honor is the very least our country can do.

No doubt Byron remembered that day for the rest of his life. I know he watched the DVD hundreds of times. It went down in the history of his life as one of the proudest days he ever spent. I saw it in his face every time he talked about it.

And I'll remember it as the day the United States of America remembered and honored Technical Staff Sergeant Byron Waitcel Matthews—the day when Mr. Matthews went to Washington.

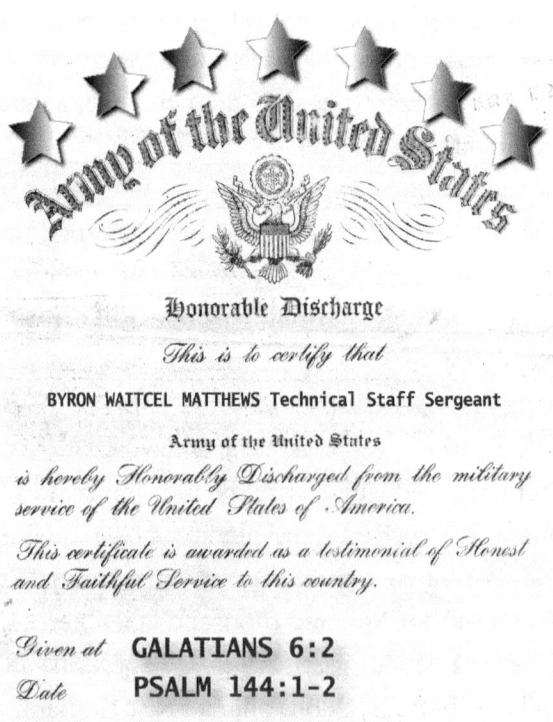

CHAPTER FIFTEEN

God Gave Me Friends So I Wouldn't Have to Deal with Harriet Oleson

EVERY SINGLE TIME I watched *Little House on the Prairie*, I found myself screaming at Harriet Oleson at the top of my lungs. For those who know the *Little House on the Prairie* TV series, Harriet is no stranger. Let me just briefly describe Harriet for those unfamiliar with her character. She's a selfish snob, along with many other bad words. Harriet and her husband, Nels, owned the Mercantile in the town of Walnut Grove. The creator of the show did an excellent job of developing this character. We'll get into some of Harriet's traits as we walk through this topic known as friendship. Suffice it to say, Harriet Oleson (fictitious or not) doesn't strike me as the type of person anyone would want to call friend. Unfortunately, I've met a few Harriets in my life.

Our character traits define us. And Harriet's traits you ask? Let's make a list: busybody, liar, snob, racist, gossiper, nag, cruel, prejudiced, hard-hearted, hard-headed, know-it-all, ignorant, selfish, unfair, simple minded, and greedy. Wow! I got carried away there for a moment.

When it comes to choosing friends we try to avoid the Harriets, but when we're young, we put little thought into things like character or moral values. It's more about whether our friends think like we do and look good in the process.

At my school, six different groups existed: the popular group, the middle of the road group (not too popular but not too goofy), wannabe hoodlums, the *real* hoodlums, wannabe nerds, and the actual I-don't-even-want-to-know-you-exist nerds.

If you fell into the middle-of-the-road category, you never, and I mean never, drifted over into wannabe nerd or actual nerd land. Doing so would wreck your image for the remainder of your school career and probably beyond. Sometimes, if you wanted to be naughty, you might be seen with one of those wannabe hoodlums.

If you wanted to be exceptionally naughty, you might even let people think you actually hung around one of the *real* hoodlums.

The popular kids pretty much stayed within their tightly knit group. They really didn't like hanging with anyone but their own kind, unless they felt supremely generous. Then they might allow a middle-of-the-roader to hang around and carry their books. Sounds very Washington, DC-ish, does it not?

Taking a hard look at the friends I've known throughout my life, I realize how very blessed I've been. That's not to say a friend never betrayed me. We all hide at least one of those in our closet of secrets. To realize a person we once trusted has, in fact, turned untrustworthy hurts terribly. It injures not only our hearts but our pride when deceit enters our life, because we all like to think of ourselves as intelligent and intuitive. But in our frail, human need for approval, we sometimes close our eyes to clues flying in front of our faces. It's easier sometimes to think, "She's my friend. She'd never hurt me." Denial is a safe place where we allow our minds to vacation.

When we find ourselves at odds with a friend, those are the times when we must draw upon our friendship and look to forgiveness. This applies when our friends wrong us or when we wrong them. One of the greatest gifts a friend ever gave me was forgiveness when I hurt her. It humbled me. I realized that forgiveness means everything in a friendship. Let's face it, human beings are sinful in nature. But the time spent building a friendship is worth cherishing by accepting that our friends, as do we, have faults. We shouldn't fall into the trap whereby we squabble with our friends and never find our way back to each other. Following my friend's lead, I made an effort to work on forgiving, as this truly isn't one of my strengths.

In elementary school, I hung around with a group who, like

me, were tomboys. We enjoyed all that goes with tree-climbing, marbles, and the like. My mother's efforts to girlify me simply didn't take at the time. Consequently my circle of friends remained quite small.

Next came middle school with all its insanity. There should be some kind of treatment for thirteen. I mean G-O-O-F can only be spelled one way. I still hung around my same friends, only at this point we kinda-sorta liked boys. In order to get them to like us back, it became necessary to act like girls. We found it silly, but it worked. And, after a while we really liked the girly girl stuff.

When high school rolled around, my family moved from one state to another. Scary time walking into a new school with no friends. Not to mention it seemed significantly larger than my hometown school. Forget getting any help from my parents. They were morons anyway. They didn't understand the teenage dilemma of going to a new school in the ninth grade. Before long I made all new friends. Life went back to being good again. The drama ended . . . well . . . sort of.

When the college years arrived, I left most of my friends behind. Sadness crept into my life once more. College presented an altogether different challenge when it came to making friends. Due to the number of students on campus, finding a friend in a sea of people who could care less about your existence proved daunting, to say the least. I learned to stick with the girls in my dorm and discovered new friends. But by this time, I knew relationships wouldn't last forever. In a way, college gets us ready for the grown-up school of friendship.

As the grown-up world came into view, I made ready to return to my high school friends. To my surprise, many either moved away, married, or had children. Throughout the years, we've all gone about our lives. Happily, through the wonders of technology, we've reconnected. But, it's not the same. It's better!

By looking back at the Harriet Olesons in my life, I appreciate my friends even more. I remember one particular girl in middle school. That's when the Harriets come out, you know. In fact, my children's book *Dealing with Margaret: Elizabeth Marie Hutchinson-When I Dream*, brings together Elizabeth and her archenemy, Margaret Callahan, the meanest girl in school.

I based the Margaret's character off the classic pre-teen Harriet. Thankfully, I only encountered her once. We were never friends. She came from money; I came from the average Joe side of the road. Her mother bought her clothes in fancy stores; my mother hand-made mine. This girl represented the snobbish, cruel, and hard-hearted traits of Harriet Olsen. When she took great delight in making fun of my clothing, one of my friends punched her in the nose. I loved it. But then, that's what friends are for.

High School brought a different type of Harriet Oleson. I made the drill team my senior year—the highlight of my entire high school career. The summer before senior year, my drill team traveled to camp, a week-long event where schools from all over the state competed. We learned several different routines and had the best time. My face hurt from laughing so much.

Towards the end of the week, each school teamed up with two other schools to choreograph a routine. Two weeks before camp, I visited Florida with a friend and her parents. My heritage is Cherokee Indian, affording me a semi-dark complexion. My friend and I spent all day, every day in the sun, and my skin became extremely dark, bordering on mahogany.

Part of the routine we learned at camp required us to raise our arms with our palms facing outward. We then touched the palm of the girl standing on either side of us. I walked over to the girl to my left, who happened to be from another school, ready to put my palm to hers. She looked at me in all my darkness of skin and said (I can remember it as if it were yesterday), "I don't touch black people."

I couldn't even respond—totally unlike me. This girl represented the racist, prejudiced, and simple-minded traits of Harriet Olsen. My team member and friend walked over and said, "She's not black, you idiot. She's Cherokee Indian!" It was fabulous. But then, that's what friends are for.

College—oh yes—my roommate. My roommate displayed the ignorant, hard-headed and selfish traits of Harriet Oleson. By the end of the semester I requested a different roommate. She started out nice enough, but halfway through the semester she turned into the demon seed. No words accurately describe her side of the room. Every night when I went to bed, I prayed something would not crawl out from under the mess on the floor and eat me alive.

She stayed out late. Even though guys weren't allowed in the dorm rooms—a dorm mom and a dorm hall captain made sure of it—this girl thought nothing of breaking any rule that didn't suit her. I feared she would bring home a drunken bum she'd found on the side of the road. She drove me mad.

One night she came home so drunk she literally crawled because she couldn't walk. Don't even ask how she got into the room. Okay, I'll tell. The guy she went out with pushed her through our bedroom window! The next morning I found her in the bathroom with her head in the toilet. No idea how that happened. I cleaned her up, changed her clothes, put her in bed—well I think it was her bed—and went on to class.

When I returned, she'd disappeared. I walked up and down the halls but couldn't find her. I went to the dorm hall captain, and asked if she knew the whereabouts of my roommate.

"Come with me," she said. We walked to the bathroom,

and there on the floor I saw my roommate, toothbrush in hand, cleaning the toilets. Evidently busted by a dorm snitch. The dorm hall captain, my friend, asked the dorm mom to let her decide my roommate's punishment. I couldn't believe it. But then, that's what friends are for.

As for the real world, the Harriet Olesons tend to run rampant. The workplace seems filled with all the Harriet traits. They hit us coming and going. Even if one doesn't work outside the home, the Harriet Olesons find a way to creep in.

Dealing with the individual Harriets tends to get a bit tedious, but it definitely builds character.

My workplace and personal Harriet Olesons faded out of my life long ago, and good riddance to them! But in their defense, they taught me a few things. One—I love my friends! Two—life is too short to dwell on the Harriet Olesons.

Here's what the Bible says about Harriet's traits:

1. *Busybody:* "We hear that some among you are idle and disruptive. They are not busy; they are busybodies. Such people we command and urge in the Lord Jesus Christ to settle down and earn the food they eat. And as for you, brothers and sisters, never tire of doing what is good" (2 Thess. 3:11–13).
2. *Snob:* "Do you see a person wise in their own eyes? There is more hope for a fool than for them" (Prov. 26:12).
3. *Racist:* "There is neither Jew nor Gentile, neither slave nor free, nor is there male and female, for you are all one in Christ Jesus" (Gal. 3:28).
4. *Gossiper:* "The mouths of fools are their undoing, and their lips are a snare to their very lives. The words of a gossip are like choice morsels; they go down to the inmost parts"

5. **Nag:** "Do not let any unwholesome talk come out of your mouths, but only what is helpful for building other up according to their needs, that it may benefit those who listen" (Eph. 4:29).
6. **Ignorant:** "Do not deceive yourselves. If any of you think you are wise by the standards of this age, you should become 'fools' so that you may become wise. For the wisdom of this world is foolishness in God's sight. As it is written: 'He catches the wise in their craftiness'; and again, 'The Lord knows that the thoughts of the wise are futile'" (1 Cor. 3:18–20).
7. **Selfish:** "But if you harbor bitter envy and selfish ambition in your hearts, do not boast about it or deny the truth. Such 'wisdom' does not come down from heaven but is earthly, unspiritual, demonic. For where you have envy and selfish ambition, there you find disorder and every evil practice" (James 3: 14–16).
8. **Greedy:** "For the love of money is a root of all kinds of evil. Some people, eager for money, have wandered from the faith and pierced themselves with many griefs" (1 Tim. 6:10).

Because the Bible is so clear on these points, we understand the importance of friendships and keeping friends close. Even if our friends don't live in the same town, or even the same state, the Internet is here to stay—thanks to that guy who invented it!

Those I've chosen to call my friends are those I've chosen to love, appreciate, cherish, confide in, stand by, and fight for all the days of my life. I worry when I see kids take friendship for granted, flaunt their rage against each other on videos, and post them on the Internet for the world to view. I worry that my granddaughters will lose sight of their friends because of pressures from those around them who don't understand what true friendship means. I worry about the women in this country who lack a trusted and faithful friend.

My mother lived well into her nineties. I saw the pain in her face when she learned that yet another one of her friends died, and she couldn't be there to say good-bye.

Choosing friends, losing friends, and forgiving friends are processes we go through as we travel the road of life together. Hopefully, along the way we choose keepers—friends for life. It brings to mind John 15:13: "Greater love has no one than this: to lay down one's life for one's friends."

While looking back at the different stages in my life, God taps me on the shoulder and says, "Remember the meaning of friend? Now look." As I run those precious faces through my mind, those wonderful friends I've grown to love and cherish, I hear myself saying out loud—"God gave me friends so I wouldn't have to deal with Harriet Oleson!"

CHAPTER SIXTEEN

Dare to tell the Truth

IDEALLY, WHEN SOMEONE ASKS a question, they receive the truth in reply. Right? Truth—that's a pretty big deal. But sometimes the truth is hard to hear—and hard to tell. It all depends on who does the telling, and who does the hearing.

My husband and I have three daughters. As children, they knew the best way to get on Mom and Dad's bad side was to lie. We gave out our most severe punishments for lying. Our oldest daughter lied terribly. Not that she told lies constantly, but that she told lies poorly. If this kid thought a lie would fit or somehow get her out of trouble, she would tell it. And it didn't matter how the lie sounded either, because she never thought through her story. Her favorite line: "Mom, I know in my heart I'm telling the truth."

For example, she loved chocolate—still does. When she found chocolate chips in the refrigerator, she always ate them without permission. She knew I planned to use them in chocolate-chip cookies, but she lacked willpower. The chocolate chips kept calling her name.

One weekend I went to the fridge all ready to make a batch of chocolate-chip cookies only to find the bag mysteriously absent. I finally discovered it placed ever so neatly on the bottom shelf, way in the back of the fridge. The bag held two—yes, count them—two chocolate chips. One stuck in each corner. I didn't need to think long to know which one of my kids devoured the entire bag, so I proceeded to summon the little darling downstairs. This kid stood in front of me, smiling from ear to ear, and asked how *she* could help *me*. To which I asked about the chocolate chips.

"Well, I didn't eat them," she responded.

I reminded her of the penalty for lying in our house. She persisted. "I didn't eat them."

I asked if that was her final word.

"Mom, I know in my heart I'm telling the truth."

With that, I took her by the shoulders, walked her to the bathroom, and faced her toward the mirror. To her surprise the cute little face looking back at her was covered in chocolate.

Two things a liar must remember:

1. Always cover your tracks.
2. Make sure you clean your face.

Our middle daughter didn't lie very often, but when she did—well—all I can say is this kid didn't just lie, she constructed the lie from the ground up and included all the plumbing and electrical work. If we found ourselves not paying attention to the story, or if we didn't ask the right questions, we never knew she was lying. That's how well she lied. Scary! However, God takes care of parents dealing with a kid clearly smarter than they.

For example, we discovered our daughter needed glasses. In order to make the experience less traumatic for her, we decided to allow her to pick out her own frames. We wanted her experience to be a good one, in spite of—kids at school and all. We planned a day of it. The entire family went along for moral support. We went to lunch and then off to the optical store. She decided on an exceptionally red pair of glasses. Yes, I know. So in an attempt to make her feel as though she made a wise choice, we all applauded her decision. She swelled with pride.

The glasses cost a pretty penny, so we told her to be very careful not to break them. Looking back, that's probably where we made our first mistake. Because break them she did, while playing a game of four square. The ball bounced up and hit her right in the face knocking the glasses to the ground. All our words about being careful, not breaking the glasses, and the cost of them swirled around her head. What to do, what to do.

Lie!

But what kind of lie? Ahh hah! A convincing one! And thus

the construction of the lie began.

One boy at her school made it his life's work to torment her throughout that year. This accident gave her the perfect opportunity to pay him back. Our daughter decided to use this boy as her scapegoat, to get her out of the situation she knew would only lead to punishment. He deserved it anyway. Always picking on girls and, in particular, picking on her. So she set him up to take the fall.

Once she told us her story, words flew between my husband and a seemingly unconcerned teacher. Anger sent us directly to the principal who promised to discipline the boy. With that, we thought the matter settled.

Several days later we learned another teacher happened to see the boy on the other side of the playground at the time, saving this kid from an unjust punishment. Needless to say, we uncovered the lie and meted out the penalty. Our daughter thought long and hard in future years before choosing the path of the lie.

Our youngest daughter couldn't bring herself to lie on a regular basis. She watched the fallout from her older sisters' escapades. She knew she didn't want to go through the same pain. When she did attempt to lie, we would say, "Are you lying?" She would smile and confess, "Yep." How do you punish that? Well, we sent her to her room to think about why she attempted the lie and warned her that trying again would result in a more severe outcome. She chose the path of truth—most times.

Now all these years later, our daughters know the importance of telling the truth. They've grown into magnificent women with high standards. More importantly they love honesty, integrity, and sincerity. I'm very proud of them.

But when I gaze out into the world, I find my daughters in the minority. Daring to tell the truth, even when it hurts, seems abnormal.

The Bible speaks to telling the truth and telling lies. Zechariah 8:16–17 tells us what the Lord expects of us as it pertains to truth. It reads: "These are the things you are to do: Speak the truth to each other, and render true and sound judgment in your courts; do not plot evil against each other, and do not love to swear falsely. I hate all this, declares the Lord." It's most likely better to seek the side God loves than the side God hates.

Romans 2:8–9 also tells us if we are self-seeking and don't tell the truth that we'll meet God's wrath and anger.

Everyone knows the adage; "The truth will set you free." That comes from John 8:31–32: "To the Jews who had believed him, Jesus said, 'If you hold to my teaching, you are really my disciples. Then you will know the truth, and the truth will set you free.'" Imagine that. All this time we've all been quoting Jesus. You gotta love it.

For me, the book of Psalms contains some of the most beautiful passages in the entire Bible. When looking for God's perspective on most anything, the book of Psalms lays out the words in such a manner as to touch the very soul. Consequently, the message of telling the truth is most eloquently written in Psalm 15:1–5: "Lord, who may dwell in your sacred tent? Who may live on your holy mountain? The one whose walk is blameless, who does what is righteous, who speaks the truth from their heart; whose tongue utters no slander, who does no wrong to a neighbor, and casts no slur on others; who despises a vile person but honors those who fear the Lord; who keeps an oath even when it hurts, and does not change their mind; who lends money to the poor without interest; who does not accept a bribe against the innocent. Whoever does these things will never be shaken." Good stuff.

One of the hardest things a person can do in life comes down to speaking the truth and keeping one's oath, even when it hurts. I call it taking a stance. When done, one can't be shaken. It says so in the passages from the book of Psalms. Standing on truth, no matter the consequences, puts us on a firm foundation. Lies tend to fall apart. Those who don't lie don't need to remember bits and pieces of the lie.

I find myself particularly frustrated when watching interviews with political figures who can't just answer questions truthfully without all the rhetoric. All too many times I hear myself screaming at the television, "A simple yes or no! Can't you just answer the question yes or no?"

History shows many political, sports, and celebrity figures who swore to tell the truth and lied. Some paid the price for lying and some didn't. Seems to me if you lie under oath, regardless of your status, you pay the price. The words that come out of our mouths reflect the character within. Everyone from every walk of life, whether in front of a camera or not, should strive toward honesty and truth.

When we take an oath or vow to do the right thing, I often wonder if we understand oath and vow mean the same. A person takes an oath of office, and we take our vows in marriage. We promise and pledge—we make a commitment to tell the truth and to answer the questions asked.

The Book of Matthew throws up more challenges to me than I even care to entertain. But I know within my soul I must. As it pertains to oaths and vows, I find it in my best interest to pay attention when Jesus speaks.

Matthew 5: 33–37 reads: "Again, you have heard that it was said to the people long ago, 'Do not break your oath, but fulfill to the Lord the vows you have made.' But I tell you, do not swear an oath at all: either by heaven, for it is God's throne; or by the earth, for it is his footstool; or by Jerusalem, for it is the city of the Great King. And do not swear by your head, for you cannot make even one hair white or black. All you need to say is simply 'Yes' or 'No'; anything beyond this comes from the evil one."

Keeping up with a lie is a most difficult task. Telling the hard truth challenges us at best. And yet God implores us to tell the truth at all times, regardless of our status in this life. The same way my husband and I pressed upon our girls to always tell the truth. In return, we owe it to our children to be truthful.

I've always believed the part of the heart that knows the waking from the dream is where the truth lives. If truth finds its way to the bottom of our priority list, we will all suffer. The question still remains, will you dare to tell the truth? A simple yes or no will do.

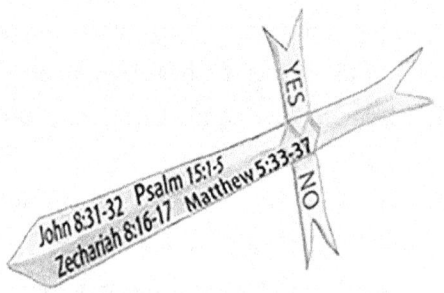

John 8:31-32 Psalm 15:1-5
Zechariah 8:16-17 Matthew 5:33-37

CHAPTER SEVENTEEN

My Daddy's Truck

MY DADDY'S TIME EFFICIENT way of teaching me something sounded like this—"Here, now do it." Daddy's cousin and her husband owned a lake house we visited every summer during my childhood. I remember it as a great place to play and relax. I remember all the fun times together. Well, except for the swimming thing.

At the age of eight, I still didn't know how to swim. I was embarrassed about this because most of my friends could swim. Some even knew how to dive. I never learned to dive, but, hey, I can float for hours. This particular summer we visited the lake house, and I told Daddy I wanted to learn how to swim.

"Great, let's go out to the dock."

All the way to the dock I almost couldn't contain my excitement.

Somewhere in the back of my mind I'm sure I wondered why we were going to the dock instead of just walking straight out into the lake. You may call me clueless!

So we walked out on the dock with me grinning from ear to ear, ready to learn how to swim. Daddy picked me up and promptly threw me in the lake. Ever heard the expression "Sink or Swim." Yep, I started swimming. My mother, who stood back on the shore watching, fainted.

My daddy just stood there and smiled. Why? Because he was a sadist and a child abuser and a crazy person! Not at all. He knew something most people don't. Survival is a powerful motivator. It's instinctive. My daddy knew I wouldn't sink. He knew I would swim. He also knew if he spent time in the water with me and went through the motions of showing me how to swim, I probably would have learned—eventually. But only after hours of screaming and crying. Being thrown off the dock left me no time for screaming and crying. I only had time to stay alive. And that's exactly what I did.

Consequently, I swam, leaving time to spend hours in the lake—swimming! If I'd been one of those people standing behind the door when God handed out the survival instinct, there's no doubt in my mind Daddy would have jumped in after me. But he expected me to swim and I did. Still, if I needed him, he was there for me.

When I turned fifteen years old, knowing how to drive became key in order to get my driver's license. No, he didn't put me in a car and run me off a dock, but I'm sure he thought about it. Worse yet, he bought a brand new 1967 Chevy truck. It gets better. Not just a new truck, a puke-green truck. Wait, it gets even better.

He bought this truck then had the audacity to redneck it up! He put a redneck camper on it and hung his rifle inside the cab. Fifteen is the age where the very fact my parents breathed embarrassed me. See the child abuse? The truck also came with no power steering, no power brakes, no power windows, no power seats, and no air conditioning. It barely even sported a radio. My daddy chose this vehicle as the tool he intended to use to teach me how to drive. Boggles the mind, right?

I probably weighed seventy-five pounds dripping wet at the time and stood not more than four feet tall. And this man wanted me to drive his redneck, no power brakes, no power steering, and no power anything puke-green truck? Yes. He did.

Did he have any sort of plan to make my feet reach the gas and brake pedals? And even if he did, how did he imagine I would be able to stop the stupid thing? No power brakes, remember? Any plan to make me strong enough to be able to turn a corner? I think not! No power steering, remember?

The nightmare started one Saturday morning shortly after my fifteenth birthday. Days before I'd gotten my learner's license. My mother gave us a list of errands to run. Daddy came to my room and said, "Let's go."

Man of many words. Let's go? Let's go where? Let's go shopping so I can buy you an entire new wardrobe? Let's go to Six Flags and you can invite as many friends as you want? I knew better. I also knew when my daddy said, "Let's go," or anything else, I did it.

I decided to play dumb. I walked outside and headed directly for my mother's car. My daddy just looked at me. You know the look. *"Good try, kiddo, now get in the truck."* No point in pulling the drama card. I needed to accept my fate.

To say I hated that truck would be an understatement. I rarely rode in it. When I did, I hid out of sight. The thought of one of my friends seeing me in that contraption put undue stress on my poor little teenaged brain.

My daddy could never be described as a sensitive sort of guy. He *never* got in touch with his feminine side. In fact, if anyone ever suggested he might have a feminine side, he would have decked them. This character trait made him totally incapable of being sensitive to my fear of friends seeing me riding around in that thing.

He could have cared less about feelings.

He intended that truck for one purpose and one purpose only: to teach me how to drive.

We lived in Atlanta at the time, and even in 1967 the highways stayed busy. Saturdays were no different. When teaching a teenager how to drive, or anyone for that matter, one would think the teacher would take that new driver out in a field somewhere or possibly to an abandoned parking lot. The reason for this is obvious. There are no other cars around for the new driver to run into! Not my daddy. Nope, he drove us to the busiest freeway in the city. A person would need to be from Atlanta or live there for a while to understand the drivers. There are no words.

Nevertheless, my daddy decided this would be the perfect place for my first driving lesson. As Daddy pulled over, panic set in. The time arrived for me to drive the vehicle I hated most in the world. Then this man, the man I called Daddy, had the unmitigated gall to look at me with a straight face and say, "Get behind the wheel."

He got out of the stupid, puke-green, redneck truck, walked around to my side, and opened the door. At that moment, I clearly understood the term "paralyzed with fear."

I got out and walked around the truck, all the while praying none of my friends would pass by. Did I have time to run down the street to call Child Protective Services? Probably not.

In all my distress, I got behind the wheel and to my surprise I actually reached the pedals. Who knew? My daddy knew.

"Start the engine," Daddy said.

I started the engine.

"Turn the wheel."

No power steering, remember? I struggled to turn the wheel.

"You can do it," said Daddy. And so I did.

"Put on your blinker."

I put on the blinker.

"Check your mirrors for traffic."

I checked my mirrors for traffic—amazingly clear.

"Slowly press on the accelerator."

I slowly pressed on the accelerator.

"Pull onto the expressway."

I pulled onto the expressway.

"Now drive."

And so I did. I drove my daddy's puke-green, redneck truck—and I loved it!

Daddy always laughed at that story. He would say, "You should have seen how Jean (that's what he called me) stopped that old truck. Whenever she stopped it, she would have to literally stand up on the brake. Yep, she was a sight to behold."

I knew Daddy expected me to follow his directions and trust him. But first I needed to make the effort. Sadly some parents don't require their kids to make an effort. Just like when he threw me off the dock. He tossed me into a situation where I needed to think for myself and react. And I did—both times.

Yes, indeed, Daddy had a way about him. He either liked you or he didn't. He saw no gray areas. Daddy saw a right side or a wrong side. You either did it or you didn't. Comprehending those concepts baffled me. Gray areas were easier. As I've gotten older, I've realized he desperately tried to teach me something else in his own way—his very military way.

He wanted me to understand what appears in Amos 5:18–19: "Woe to you who long for the day of the Lord! Why do you long for the day of the Lord? That day will be darkness, not light. It will be as though a man fled from a lion only to meet a bear, as though he entered his house and rested his hand on the wall only to have a snake bite him." My daddy wanted me to be prepared when challenges came my way. He wanted me to know how to deal with the bear, if and when I fled from the lion. And he wanted me to guard against becoming so comfortable in my surroundings that I paid no attention to the snake lurking about.

Daddy owned that truck throughout my teenage years. He kept it after I became an adult with children of my own. As much as I hated that redneck truck, my kids loved it. They loved sitting in it. But one day, while Daddy and I chatted, they climbed inside unnoticed, and somehow hit the gearshift. We heard a strange sound, turned, and saw the truck rolling down the driveway.

Daddy immediately started running after it. The door on the driver's side flew opened and we saw my youngest daughter trying to get out. Without hesitation, my middle daughter grabbed her by the arm and pulled her back inside.

Just as the truck started rolling out into the street, Daddy grabbed the opened door, jumped inside, and slammed on the brakes. This all happened within a matter of seconds. I stood frozen, feet glued to the concrete. Then I heard Daddy's bellowing laugh. *He's gone insane!* I remember thinking. *My kids could have died!* But then I always knew he was crazy. Remember the dock? Remember the driving lesson?

I went running down the driveway vowing to put my lunatic of a father in an asylum. As I threw open the passenger's door my middle daughter, who'd just saved her little sister's life, looked at me and said, "Mommy, Papa's truck saved our lives."

"I wuv Papa's twuck," my youngest daughter announced. My daddy started laughing again.

He knew I hated that truck, and he knew that I knew that he knew. What's that ridiculous saying? "He who laughs first laughs last." I guess payback time had arrived for all the times I made fun of that truck.

It's interesting how over time, things and I guess even people you really dislike come to grow on you. From the moment I laid eyes on that truck I hated every stinkin' inch of it. Still, I drove it from time to time. I just made sure I didn't go anywhere near my friends. But, then, that too faded away as I became less embarrassed by it.

The day finally came when Daddy couldn't drive anymore. The truck sat in the driveway for several years. One day, my mother decided it needed to go. Daddy didn't fight her. He loved that truck too much to watch it rot away in the driveway.

Sometimes I believe God looks down on us from heaven and laughs at our quirks—our loves, our hates, our passions, our disappointments, our trials, our errors, and our joys. He knows our strengths and weaknesses and doesn't test us beyond what we can endure. Kinda like my daddy knew.

My mother called to say she found someone who wanted to buy the truck. I laughed when she said their mailman made an offer. He noticed it sitting in my parents' driveway for years. He said he always wanted it. Go figure.

The day my mother sold that stupid, puke-green, redneck truck felt like one of the saddest days of my life—for no other reason than it was my daddy's truck.

CHAPTER EIGHTEEN

Remembering Will Have to Do

REMEMBERING UNCLE BUCK. NOT an easy task for me. Uncle Buck lost his life at the ripe young age of thirty-six, in the year of our Lord 1966. That made him one year older than my youngest child is now. My sweet heaven—one year *older* than my youngest child.

A senseless car accident ripped him out of our lives a month after my fourteenth birthday. Uncle Buck meant the world to me. He lived life to the fullest. He didn't deserve to die.

Almost every summer as a kid, I visited my papa and grandma. They spoiled me rotten, which is the main reason I liked visiting. What do you expect from a kid? Kids are shallow and materialistic. But the *real* reason I loved visiting Papa and Grandma was because Uncle Buck lived there.

He was tall and skinny with short, curly brown hair. He appeared to be eight feet tall. Or that's how it seemed to me. Our times together were magical. He took me everywhere. I had just turned eight when he took me to the state fair. The sights and sounds made my head spin. Consequently, I got lost. We were both frantic until we found each other. I thought Uncle Buck would beat my behind, but he didn't. He hugged me until I thought my eyes were going to pop out of my head, and then he bought me a cotton candy. The man possessed zero parenting skills. Who cared? He was my Uncle Buck.

I remember most his patience. Job comes to mind. He needed patience, dealing with a kid like me. But Uncle Buck showed patience with everyone.

My grandma suffered from severe diabetes. She took insulin shots. She lost almost all her toes due to the diabetes. Some days, pain wreaked havoc on her poor body, but she never complained. That's the part I remember about her the most—her graciousness. A true lady for sure.

I can remember being six or seven years old when the diabetes started taking its toll on Grandma's body. When she lost her toes, walking became difficult, so Uncle Buck helped her. He bathed her, combed her hair, changed her bed linens. He treated her feet and changed the bandages. The ritual took hours. It involved soaking her feet in medication, cleaning the wounds (wounds that would never heal), and then applying a special liquid medication on them before bandaging them again.

Uncle Buck always let me help. He called me his little helper. I couldn't imagine anything cooler than helping Uncle Buck help my grandma. When I think back over that time, I can close my eyes and see my grandma's bedroom. I can smell the medications Uncle Buck so lovingly applied to Grandma's feet.

Uncle Buck never married. He devoted his life to Grandma. Being quite the looker, he never lacked for female attention. He dated but nothing more. He enjoyed his guy friends and hung with them, but his priority never shifted from Grandma.

Of course, Papa never strayed very far from Grandma's side, either. He just didn't have the stomach to care for her medically. He cared for her in other ways—the kind of care a husband gives to his wife.

I'm sure my visits were disruptive. Most times I could be found bugging Uncle Buck or Grandma. I loved to comb her long, beautiful, straight black hair. I could sit for hours combing it, and she allowed me to, regardless of how she felt at the time. I guess Uncle Buck got his patience from her. Papa would step in, to Grandma's relief I'm sure, though she never let on, and shuffle me outside so Grandma could rest. As I look back over my childhood, my visits with Uncle Buck, Papa, and Grandma are by far my happiest memories.

When I turned nine, Grandma died—July 24, 1961. I cried for

a long time. Uncle Buck cried too, but he held me in his arms and told me Grandma went to heaven. He said God made Grandma His special angel. I still miss her.

Then on June 25, 1966, Uncle Buck died. I died some that day too. The local paper reported the car accident as the worst in the history of North Carolina. Three out of the four men in the car died.

The man driving the car was drunk. Uncle Buck and the other two men tried desperately to stop him from getting behind the wheel, but he refused to listen. To this very day I don't understand why Uncle Buck didn't take the man's keys or just walk away. Instead, they all got into the car. That decision cost them their lives—with the exception of the fourth guy—the guy who lived to tell about it.

The accident report indicated the car was traveling in excess of a hundred miles per hour. The driver lost control while going around a curve. The car traveled 688 feet, ran into a ditch, hit a culvert, then flew through the air for eighty-five feet, uprooted a pine tree, then landed on a parked car.

Due to the massive impact, the driver went through the driver's side window. The passenger sitting up front went through the passenger's side window. Uncle Buck, seated in the back seat, went through the front windshield. The fourth guy suffered a broken arm and a few other injuries. They weren't wearing seatbelts. I don't know for sure if this car even had seatbelts.

All I know is when we received the news of my Uncle Buck's death I, at the age of fourteen, declared war on God.

We later learned the fourth guy paid a visit to Papa when he got out of the hospital. He told Papa when the driver started going so fast, they all tried to get him to slow down. But he wouldn't. He also told Papa Uncle Buck said, "We're all going to die."

This man, the youngest of the four, idolized my Uncle Buck. He followed him everywhere. So when Uncle Buck told him to get down in the floor of the car and hold on to whatever he could find, he did. Then he looked over at Uncle Buck and saw him praying. But he wasn't asking God to save them. He was simply praying "The Lord's Prayer." The man who survived started praying along with him.

When the car went around that curve, this guy said he felt Uncle Buck shielding him. The next thing he knew, he woke up in the hospital. My Uncle Buck saved his life.

The two years following Uncle Buck's death, I raged against God. I always heard adults say, "God is in control. It's all in God's hands. God has a plan." Well, I thought, if all that's true, why did my Uncle Buck die? Why didn't God stop him from getting in that car in the first place? Why didn't He make Uncle Buck the one to survive instead of some guy I didn't even know? Why did He let it happen at all?

As I look back on my rage now, the anger I thought I felt for God I really felt toward Uncle Buck. If I'd realized that at fourteen, the devastation would have sent me reeling. I believe God protected me from that realization until I could understand the true root of my anger.

When my papa told me the story of the guy who survived, my rage extended to this guy I didn't know. In my mind, it became his fault too. Adding him into my realm of anger made it easier to bear. My anger toward Uncle Buck remained hidden. Now I could blame God and this guy. My Uncle Buck died. Someone should take the blame. It might as well be God and this stranger.

Papa said, "Child, Buck was a hero. He gave his life for his friend. Don't you see, child? Grandma needed Buck. And I believe God brought them back together in heaven. And some day we will all meet again. What a glorious day that will be child. What a glorious day that will be."

I needed time to realize who deserved my rage. In the end, no one did—not even the guy driving the car. It took a while for me to get to that point. During that time, I held back from God. I needed to blame Him more than Uncle Buck. Uncle Buck was flesh and blood to me. I could touch him. I could look at his face and know he existed. With God, I needed faith. Besides, how could I ever betray Uncle Buck, the man I adored, by blaming him? So I didn't. God was just an easier target. I could dump all my anger at His doorstep. I figured He didn't care anyway.

They say with a little age comes wisdom. Well, maybe. All I know is that God waited patiently for me because He knew the teachings Uncle Buck left behind. He knew it would only be a matter of time. He was right. God's plan was laid out for me. He sent another special guy to show me how much His love for us is ever present in our lives. No matter the pain.

As the years passed, Uncle Buck became a sweet memory of my childhood, a good guy who died at a very young age. He touched my life in ways I'll never forget. He taught me patience, which I've yet to master. He taught me to show kindness to others. He taught me the meaning of friendship. He taught me to honor and respect the older generation. But more than any of those things he taught me the meaning of unconditional love.

In 1 Corinthians 13:4 we read: "Love is patient, love is kind. It does not envy, it does not boast, it is not proud." Those words healed my heart through the years. Uncle Buck was the best of the best. I miss him still—even after all these years.

As I think back over the people in my life who now spend their days with the Lord, I say a prayer for those they've left behind. I know we will meet again and like my papa said, "What a glorious day that will be." So I offer up their names as a reminder of their presence on this earth. In memory of:

Claude Calloway Stone	Buck Bell
Luther J. Bell	Hattie Bell
L.J. Bell	Worth Bell
Albert Bell	Buddy Bell
Dessi Bell	Bennie Locklear
Ruby Locklear	Kay Bell
Virginia Oxendine	Anthony Oxendine
Sarah Lois Bell	Jack Bell
Ella Morgan Stone	Tyler David Bernard
Willie Oxendine	Maggie J. Oxendine
William Calloway Stone	Michelle Alwert
Jan Hundley	Kevin Kepner
Cindy Philmon Walker	Evelyn Galloway
Virginia Whisenant	Harry Whisenant
Charlie Sineath	Margaret Williams
Rachel Williams	Larry Matthews
Kay Matthews	Mercer Matthews
Mertice Matthews	Marge Skinner
Mary Barfield	Bobby Burch
Beth Buzzard	Katherine Boland
Steve Boland	Doris Oxendine
Howard Oxendine	Bert Morgan
Gladys Morgan	Annie Bell Weeks
Mary Mull	Mickey Matthews
Marian Philmon	Bob Philmon
Granny Russell	Earl Peeler
Max Holland	Lisa Pritchard
Melba Shipp	Frances Selfridge

Judy Matthews	Mrs. Mary Ray
Judd Hodges	Ted Wall
Karl Smith	Susan Head
Jean Poole	L.G. Morgan
Michael Leff	Mickie Parker
Sharon L. Kilman	Iona Tuley
Ruth Williams Bolton	Baby McDonald
Emma Grace McDonald	Margie Griffin
Doris Fair	E.M. Funderburke
Chuck Skinner	Nicole Raye Bell Stade
Evelyn Bell Stone	Nancy Rives
Lynda Innes Taylor	

They were all too young to die. Not just in age, but because we weren't done loving them yet. It's the letting go that scars the heart. It's the saying goodbye that stings the eyes. I miss them all. So until we meet again dear ones—remembering will have to do.

"He will wipe every tear from their eyes. There will be no more death or mourning or crying or pain, for the old order of things has passed away." Revelation 21:4

CHAPTER NINETEEN

Where in the World Did That
Hair on My Chin Come From?

AT THE AGE OF sixteen, my girlfriends and I used to sit around and talk about our mothers and how we were never going to grow up looking, acting, or smelling like them. We couldn't imagine turning out like our mothers—or any other woman our mother's age, for that matter. Words like gross, disgusting, creepy, hideous, nasty, and nauseating all crossed our minds.

I remember writing a list of things I hated most about my mother's appearance. Her square butt, double chin, scrawny little fingers, pitiful little fingernails, and toothpick legs really annoyed me. I also noticed my friends' mothers, and they seemed worse than mine. Some of these women even sported a mustache! Some had hair on their chins. Some seemed to be in a constant state of sweat. How they ever went out in public I never understood.

However, as we grow older, and sometimes wiser, we develop a new-found respect for our mothers. We now see the world through their eyes. If we are fortunate and our mothers are still with us, we tend to forge a new relationship with them.

We all recognize, whether our mothers are with us or not, that yes, they were right all along. It suddenly clicks as we watch our own off-spring act as we did. But when we're sixteen, we look at the exterior of a person because looks are everything. No opinion of the same sex or opposite sex is based on anything other than appearance. We're sixteen. We're basically nitwits. Therefore, at that age, I couldn't imagine a future that looked like my mother.

Little did I know.

My oldest daughter walked in on me in the bathroom one day. She was about five years old at the time. It happened to be that time of the month for me. You know when *Aunt Flo* comes to visit? I never minded Aunt Flo's visits because it meant I wouldn't experience the pleasure of another five-year-old bursting into the bathroom anytime soon, and the bathroom seemed the only place I could enjoy just a little fraction of time alone. When one is a mother, privacy ceases to exist. Along with modesty.

Anyway, the kid came crashing in (now keep in mind I'm at the halfway point of—you know—changing), and upon seeing what's going on, she proceeded to scream at the top of her lungs, "Mommy! What are you doing?" Moments with our children are so special, aren't they? I very discreetly continued on with, you know, all the while trying to explain to her what she saw. Age appropriateness is highly overrated in my view.

At the end of the explanation, my five-year-old, in all her years of experience and wisdom, said, "That's never happening to me!"

"Well, dear, yes it will."

"No, it won't 'cause I won't let it!"

"Well, dear, I'm afraid you have no control over it. It happens to every girl."

"Not me!"

Never get into an argument with a five-year-old. You won't win.

My daughter went on to bless us with three grandchildren. I'm not a gambling person, but I would be willing to bet she welcomes Aunt Flo's visit every month now.

The relationship we share with older women, whether they are our mothers, aunts, or even friends' mothers is a strange one. During my teenage years, the thought of turning out like one of these older creatures terrified me. I remember checking out my butt to make sure it didn't look like my mother's. Yet I soon realized I would never escape the inevitability of my butt looking just as square as hers. How could it not? All my aunts had square butts. Even my uncles had square butts. Let's face it; we were a family of square-butted people. I was doomed.

After the butt obsession ended, my next concern revolved around my chin. I feared it would develop into my mother's double chin. To my dismay, that's exactly what happened. No matter how skinny I became, this double-chin thing still plagued me.

As for my mother's toothpick legs, well, I escaped that one. At one point, I thought I'd escaped the scrawny little fingers as well, but one day I looked at my hands and saw my mother's scrawny little fingers, pitiful fingernails, and all. Come to think of it, the only time my nails were ever descent-looking happened during pregnancy. So much for that idea.

We all look at older women when we're young and, like my five-year-old daughter, we say, "That's *never* happening to me!" But happen it does, and yes dear, we can't control it. Most of us realize that God possesses a sense of humor. It's called menopause! Not funny! I'm *not* laughing.

Age makes our boobs and our butts droop. It's an unfortunate fact of life. There's plastic surgery, but what woman in her right mind does that? The majority of those who do go under the knife come out looking like silly putty that's been stretched beyond recognition. Let's face it, plastic surgeons can only stretch the skin so far until the patient looks like a creature from the Black Lagoon. Not for me. I'll just deal with the normal progression of age—underarm wings and all.

Underarm wings—yuck! That's another aging thing I believed only overweight old women developed. It's not something I ever intended to allow to happen to my body. Then one summer while my granddaughters visited, my husband took them for a Papa outing. He likes to take them out by himself for the day and buy them a shopping mall. It's so cute.

Anyway, I walked them out to the car, made sure they were all seat-belted in, kissed them goodbye, and wished them a wonderful time. In the summertime, my husband likes to roll the windows down in the car, turn the radio up full blast, and make a fool out of himself. He particularly likes it when our daughters or granddaughters are in the car with him because it embarrasses them beyond belief. It does absolutely nothing to him. He's beyond embarrassment. He knows not to do it with me. We sleep together, and he fears for his life and other body parts.

As they backed out of the driveway, I raised my arm to wave goodbye and my oldest granddaughter stuck her head out the window and yelled, "Grandma, your underarm is shaking!" Then she burst into laughter. *Not* funny, you little creep. The thing that would never happen to me happened. There I stood with the square-butt family curse hovering overhead and now the underarm wing thing just attached itself to my body. How much more could possibly happen?

Ever wonder what happens to leg hair as you age? After the age of sixty, you wonder about these things. I discovered what happens to it. It comes out in other parts of your body! Recently I've noticed that it's not necessary to shave my legs as often as I used to. Why? Because it's growing out of my face!

Excessive facial hair used to appear in my nightmares. It all went back to the time when I noticed my friend's mother's goatee. There were rumors she might be the bearded lady in the circus. We used to laugh at that thought. Not so funny now.

I now believe the adage "What goes around comes around," and it comes around in a big way. Needless to say, I became that which I mocked. I believe there really is a mother's curse, and that my mother put the curse on me. I, in turn, put the curse on my daughters. That's our only salvation, you know. It allows us to deal with what's happening to our own bodies. We eventually get to watch our kids deal with it too, which is always fun!

We never think, when we're young, that we're in the best part of our lives. All we want is to grow older, which sometimes ain't all it's cracked up to be. But we don't want to look like our mothers. And we especially don't want to act like them.

I used to visit an assisted-living facility once a month as a part of my church's Caring Ministry program. Before my first visit, the church sent me a list of the dos and don'ts regarding visitation. It rattled me so much I almost stayed home. I didn't feel qualified for this job. I needed some kind of an "old-age visitors" degree. I contacted my instructor who told me not to worry—just be myself. As long as I possessed a caring heart, everything would be fine. She must be kidding. The list took up two pages. I needed to go back to college for this. Did I think this through before I signed up for this task? A place in heaven maybe? Not really. I just wanted to give back a little, and I thought visiting the elderly would be a good start.

Two ladies were assigned to me. Through this wonderful ministry, I received more of a blessing than I could ever imagine. I developed a wonderful relationship with one of the ladies. Unfortunately, the other lady became ill. They moved her to a nursing home after I'd only visited with her once. Yet I felt like I lost a friend. My mind drifted back to the sixteen-year-old that would throw up at the idea of visiting an old person. It seems quite silly now. Outward appearances are now replaced with inward beauty.

As it turned out, I made more of the dos and don'ts list than it deserved. What I learned from my new friend—this sweet precious "elderly" lady—is that life is a gift God gives us. Inside that gift are memories. Memories we share with each other, and memories we keep for ourselves. As I sat and listened to her gift box of memories, it filled me to overflowing. I realized underneath all the sagging skin and wing-flapping underarms is that special thing we all hold dear—our life's experiences. Although she's with the Lord now, I wouldn't trade the time we spent together for all the world can offer. I miss her every day.

At sixteen, it's all about appearances. Now it's all about the memories. Psalm 71:17–18 tells us: "Since my youth, God, you have taught me, and to this day I declare your marvelous deeds. Even when I am old and gray, do not forsake me, my God, till I declare your power to the next generation, your mighty acts to all who are to come." When I read those verses, I think of my friend. She brought a lot of class to "elderly," and it doesn't seem so bad anymore.

My mother came to live with us a few years ago. It's been quite an adjustment. Not because she's a terrible person to live with but because I've not lived with my mother in over thirty-seven years. In addition to that, when she came to live with us, all of my kids were grown and out of the house. I'd become very accustomed to being alone during the day. It became necessary to adjust to someone being around, to cooking for an extra person, cleaning up after an extra person, and hearing the same stories over and over again. Not to mention all the different body noises and the smell of Bengay.

I find myself looking at my elderly mother sometimes and thinking, "That's me in two years!" Seriously, I think about getting older and watching the rest of my body fall into my socks, giving up things I never thought I would need to give up or ever wanted to give up. I must say, she's done well in that regard. She's given up *things* with grace, and I'll always admire her for that.

Then the defiant part of me says, "That's never happening to me!" I look in the mirror and wonder, *where did all the years go and how did they go by so fast?* Wasn't it yesterday when I attended high school? And yesterday when I came home from the hospital with my oldest child—a mother now, with three kids of her own? And certainly it was yesterday when I had no gray hair, no wrinkles, no sagging body, no age spots, and no stiff joints.

Now when I look in the mirror I don't see an older woman. I see a vibrant young woman with her entire life in front of her. That sounds like a wonderful fantasy, doesn't it? Yet I wouldn't change a thing. As I admire the laugh lines around my eyes and mouth, which we all know are signs of a happy life, I hold my head high, proud to be me, and think—where in the world did that hair on my chin come from?

Psalm 71:17-18

CHAPTER TWENTY

Where Exactly Are the Places You Will Go?

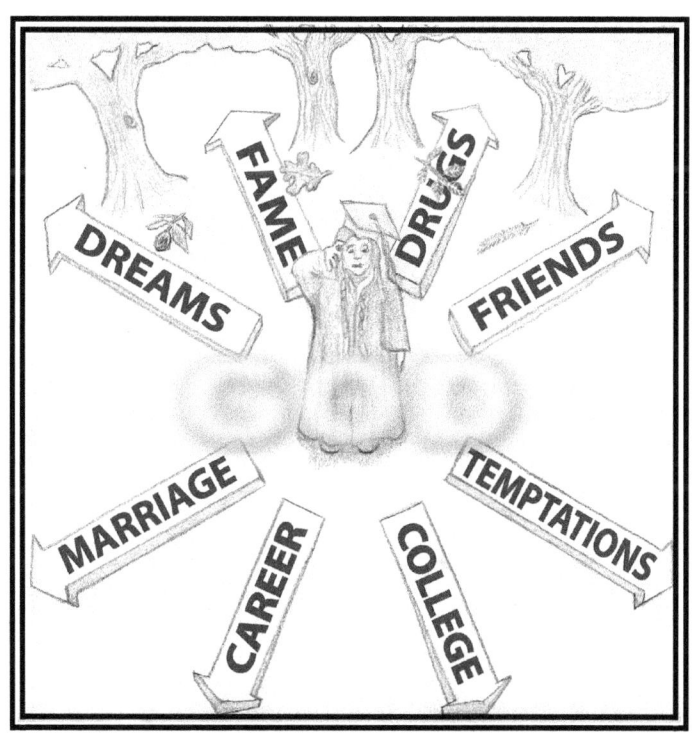

ONE MIGHT BE HARD-PRESSED to find a graduate who hasn't received the book *Oh, the Places You'll Go!* by Dr. Seuss as a graduation gift. When my youngest daughter graduated from high school, her best friend gave her this wonderful book. Now for some hard truth and I write this with great embarrassment—I never actually read the book until a little while ago. I know I know. In my defense—scratch that. There is no defense. I am so very sorry!

So why, after all these years, did I finally decide to read this book? The answer is quite simple. It's because of my next-door neighbor.

They've lived next to us for the past eighteen years. We built our houses within one month of each other. When we met, their daughter was about eight months old. Now she's a high school graduate. Amazing!

My youngest daughter, who happened to be in elementary school when we built our house, is now a third grade teacher. So when our neighbor's daughter graduated, my daughter said that she wanted to be the one to give her *Oh, the Places You'll Go!* She said she loved the book so much, and it provided a great message. A great message? I never knew that.

Being the considerate person I am, I offered to run by the bookstore and pick up a copy of the book for my daughter. Not because I thought her incapable of going to the bookstore herself. Nope. A more sinister plan brewed in the back of my mind. This would be the perfect opportunity for me to read the book, thus allowing me to flaunt my vast knowledge of its content. And read it I did. The minute I got in the car. No, I didn't read it while driving. I read it aloud to my husband while he drove.

What can I say? We were both quite impressed. He'd never read it either! How could this charming little book sit undisturbed on the bookshelf in my house all the years my daughter attended college? As they say, it's never too late to learn. My daughter was right. The book provides a wonderful message.

After reading the book, I realized I didn't know much about its author. Of course I knew *of* him, but no in-depth info. According to Dr. Seuss' website (*www.seussville.com/#/author*) he was born Theodor Seuss Geisel on March 2, 1904, in Springfield, Massachusetts. In 1925 he attended Dartmouth. In the school's humor magazine the *Jack-O-Lantern*, he published the first cartoon where he used "Seuss" as his pseudonym. In 1926 he attended Oxford. In 1928 he created his first "Quick, Henry, the Flit!" advertisement. He went on to write his first children's book. It's an ABC of fanciful creatures. But, it didn't find a publisher. Finally in 1937 *And to Think That I Saw It on Mulberry Street* became Dr. Seuss' first published children's book. In 1941 Seuss began his career as a political cartoonist. In 1984 for his body of work, Dr. Seuss won the Pulitzer Prize. Theodor Seuss Geisel died on September 24, 1991, at the age of eighty-seven. Ironically, this devoted children's book author who wrote over sixty children's books never had children of his own.

Back to *Oh, the Places You'll Go!* As I read through the book, I realized that the message is quite clear. Dr. Seuss is preparing his readers for the ups and downs of life. The message I received came down to choices and the avenues we go down throughout our life. How life can sometimes be scary but in the end, we're all capable of doing great things as long as we face our obstacles and move forward.

After completing my mission of reading *Oh, the Places You'll Go!*, I sat down to ponder the places I've gone. I realized from my own history that Dr. Seuss got it right. Things weren't easy all the time. Some places were pretty scary. Situations got very confusing. Difficult decisions made things uneasy. It ain't been a party all the time. I've made some good turns and some bad turns. I've soared, and I've crashed. I've had to learn how to balance it all out and understand I can't win all the time.

From time to time, we all need to sit down and assess the avenues in our lives. We need to look at the choices we've made. We need to remember that life, in all its glory, is difficult at best, but that challenges are the things that keep up sharp. They keep us on our toes, and hopefully we learn from them.

The biggest mistake we can make while raising our children is to coddle them. While teaching Vacation Bible School one summer, it became painfully obvious to me that the parents of this generation are the ultimate coddlers. Sad but true. In all my time of dealing with children, I've never seen a more hyper-sensitive bunch. Believe me, I'm not just talking about the kids. From time to time I found it quite disturbing to be around these kids. I found drama, and more drama, at every turn. It can get very tiresome.

Take, for example, the technology that's available to us. A person can't turn on the TV, radio, or Internet without hearing or reading about some *drama*, whether from a celebrity, a politician, or the average person. These people exaggerate the drama for the attention it gets them. The media provides them with the coddling they crave. Then they head down one of those avenues Dr. Seuss warns us about.

Certain activists feed on drama. It's what keeps them in business. They see a drama, take it to the extreme, and involve the media. The drama stars exacerbate the event, the activists chime in, and then the drama stars become even more pathetic. Then the coddling begins. And it goes on and on and on and on—until intelligent people literally become nauseated.

While reading Dr. Seuss's book, I came to respect the author who told his readers in no uncertain terms that life ain't always gonna be a bowl of cherries. How we handle those times determines the paths we choose and the character that emerges.

Dr. Seuss didn't coddle his readers. He laid truth right on the line. He encouraged us, built us up even, but he reminded us that in this life, we face challenges, and we don't always win. There's no room for being a sore loser. There's no time for self-pity. A person must face his or her demons and move forward. The paths that lay before us can, often times, be daunting. It's easier, sometimes, to choose the path we see everyone else taking. However, it's not always the right path. When parents coddle their children and make them think they'll never have to deal with the realities of life, they do a great disservice to the child.

The thing that stood out for me during my Vacation Bible School experience occurred when I walked down the halls with my group of kids. The old-aged teachers, like me, looked most bewildered. When we caught one another's eye we could literally read each other's mind. We were all saying the same thing—loudly, "What was I thinking? Where do these kids come from anyway? Is it time to go home yet?" The drama we dealt with became overwhelming. Now here comes the "but" part. But I would do it again in a second, because I loved those kids to pieces, despite our generational gap.

Remember good old Jimmy Dugan, the character in *A League of Our Own*? He said, "There's no crying in baseball." Truer words were never spoken. Maybe because I grew up the daughter of a drill sergeant, or maybe because most of my best friends were guys or maybe because I learned to suck it up at the age of two, but I've always known there's no crying in baseball.

In the course of my life, I've worked for two major corporations—both male dominated. Now I know that's a bit of the old stick-in-the-craw for my sister feminists—please—but nevertheless, it's a fact. I've witnessed every disgusting male characteristic there is to witness, and let me just say, I'm the better for it. I do not now, nor have I ever, cried in baseball. In fact, one of my friends said to me, "You *never* cry."

Here's my dirty little secret: I do cry. I just don't cry in baseball.

When I left my male-dominated corporate life and went to work for a well-known hotel in the sales and catering department, there were twenty-plus women and one poor lonely man. Pitiful, I tell you. The first week of my employment, not a day went by that some woman didn't break down in tears.

I came home every day and told my husband, "I can't take this crying. I'm about to either pull my hair out or smack one of these chicks."

"Don't do that," he said, "or they'll never stop crying."

That job lasted a little over three years. I adjusted to the crying, but it almost did me in. It did, however, teach me tolerance, which pleased God greatly.

I'm so glad my next-door neighbor's daughter graduated or I'd probably never experienced Dr. Seuss' charming little book jam-packed with the realities of life. Things just seem to work out, don't they? And I learned some facts about Dr. Seuss.

I decided that in addition to reading the book, I owed it to myself to check with my guidebook, as that's where I turn for answers and insights about life. Throughout his book, Dr. Seuss congratulates the "you," but he also speaks to trials, temptations, plans for the future, celebration, winning, losing, knowledge, unhappiness, and confidence. That's a lot of important stuff! The Bible also speaks to all of those things. Imagine that.

Pertaining to trials and temptations, I found James 1:2–8: "Consider it pure joy, my brothers and sisters, whenever you face trials of many kinds, because you know that the testing of your faith produces perseverance. Let perseverance finish its work so that you may be mature and complete, not lacking anything. If any of you lacks wisdom, you should ask God, who gives generously to all without finding fault, and it will be given to you. But when you ask, you must believe and not doubt, because the one who doubts is like a wave of the sea, blown and tossed by the wind. That person should not expect to receive anything from the Lord. Such a person is double-minded and unstable in all they do." That's powerful. No coddling or excuses.

Then there are our plans for the future. Jeremiah 29:11 tells us: "'For I know the plans I have for you,' declares the Lord, 'plans to prosper you and not to harm you, plans to give you hope and a future.'"

What about celebration? Life is made for celebration, is it not? I love celebrations, but I think we need to be aware of what we're celebrating. We should take care that we don't always celebrate the greatness of ourselves. 1 Corinthians 10:31 warns: "So whether you eat or drink or whatever you do, do it all for the glory of God." That's a tough one because sometimes we want to celebrate just to be celebrating. Or we want to celebrate our own accomplishment. We need to celebrate with the understanding that our accomplishments are a gift. That gift comes from God.

Next is winning and losing. I submit that God loves us so much that He wants us to win. It reminds me of how we as parents feel about our children. We never want them to lose. But lose, we must. Through losing, we learn and grow. The learning and growing part will never happen if our parents never allow us to fail. John 16:33 tells us: "I have told you these things, so that in me you may have peace. In this world you will have trouble. But take heart! I have overcome the world." Jesus, as does Dr. Seuss, makes it clear that we will indeed win, lose, and have tribulation.

When it comes to knowledge, Proverbs 18:15 conveys it best: "The heart of the discerning acquires knowledge, for the ears of the wise seek it out." Then in Proverbs 2:10–11 we see how knowledge is the key to our lives going in the right direction: "For wisdom will enter your heart, and knowledge will be pleasant to your soul. Discretion will protect you, and understanding will guard you."

None among us wishes to be unhappy; however, unhappiness is something we all face at one time or another. The Bible points out the course of action that leads to a solution during those times of unhappiness. In Philippians 4:6 we read: "Do not be anxious about anything, but in every situation, by prayer and petition, with thanksgiving, present your requests to God."

Finally, the subject of confidence is also addressed in the Bible. Mark 11:23 tells us: "Truly I tell you, if anyone says to this mountain, 'Go, throw yourself into the sea,' and does not doubt in their heart but believes that what they say will happen, it will be done for them."

When I've come upon the challenge of trials, temptations, plans for the future, celebration, winning, losing, knowledge, unhappiness, and confidence in my life, I remember the verse in 1 Corinthians 10:13: "No temptation has overtaken you except what is common to mankind. And God is faithful; he will not let you be tempted beyond what you can bear. But when you are tempted, he will also provide a way out so that you can endure it."

In a roundabout way, I believe Dr. Seuss also drew from that passage. No proof of that mind you, just my gut feeling. That's what I got out of his wonderful little book anyway. So I leave you with my own little verse: whether you're just starting out or moving real slow, where exactly *are* the places you will go?

THE END

(OR MAYBE NOT....)

www.ingramcontent.com/pod-product-compliance
Lightning Source LLC
LaVergne TN
LVHW051518070426
835507LV00023B/3173